LIVING
ON THE EDGE

LIVING
ON THE EDGE

CHERIE BREMER-KAMP

DAVID & CHARLES
Newton Abbot   London

To our children
Annapurna, Daniel,
Russell, Chad and Stewart,
who wondered why

PAGE 2: *Photo of Chris taken by his first climbing partner Heinz Graupe.*

British Library Cataloguing in Publication Data

Bremer-Kamp, Cherie
   Living on the edge.
   1. Mountaineering——Kanchenjunga (Nepal
   and India)   2. Kanchenjunga (Nepal and
   India)——Description and travel
   I. Title
   915.49'6   DS495.8.K26

   ISBN 0−7153−9003−1

Designed and produced by
Mead & Beckett Publishing
139 Macquarie Street, Sydney, Australia

© Cherie Bremer-Kamp 1987

Designed by Leonie Bremer-Kamp
Typeset by Setrite Typesetters, Hong Kong
Printed by Mandarin Offset Marketing (HK) Ltd,
Hong Kong for David & Charles Publishers plc
Brunel House Newton Abbot Devon

CONTENTS

1

'And I have an enemy,' I cried
'And he is terrible and strong
Stronger than ocean, wilder far,
His name is Fear, I know him well.
How should I lock him in a shell?'

ROSEMARY DOBSON

THE FIRST thing I remember was blackness as an overwhelming force pushed me backwards into the seat. Unable to resist the buffeting that followed, I gave in to it. Then perfect stillness came and cautiously I blinked my eyes open. A deep emerald green, broken by occasional bubbles of air, greeted me; fellow captives held ransom by the sea. Bottles of spice drifted by. I felt warm and undisturbed at the thought that our small vessel was probably plummeting its way to the distant ocean floor; vaguely curious to discover the sensation of salt water entering my air passages and filling my lungs. Just how long could I hold on? Suspended in time, I waited.

A sudden motion yanked me into the world of the living. As we uprighted I saw Chris, with a dazed expression, braced between the mizzenmast and bulkhead. Water poured down the stairwell and rushed past his knees like a hungry mountain stream, slurping and gurgling towards the fo'c's'le. Despair, dismay passed between us as our eyes met. 'Oh God, sweetheart, I'm so sorry,' cried Chris as we reached out to hold one another. 'How could I have got us into this?' A sweet moment passed, then, filled with an urgency for action, I wormed out of his secure embrace to scramble for a bucket. 'Here, you bail I'll pump.' Words were clipped short with tension as we frantically set to work. Almost immediately the bilge hose became clogged with debris. Chris plunged his head repeatedly into the filthy muck in an attempt to clear the hose. Finally it broke and he threw the useless thing aside in disgust. A mix of

7

diesel oil, flour and brown sugar covered the floor, along with supplies of all descriptions that had spewed forth from every conceivable corner.

Chris skated and slid his way towards the radio. 'Mayday Mayday Mayday, this is yacht *Laylah*, 40 degrees north latitude, 140 degrees west longitude.' Our position was probably close to over 1,600 km (1,000 miles) from the mainland. Could someone hear our plea for help in the middle of the north Pacific in an area of gale and storm that extended over 1,600 km (1,000 miles) wide and several hundred miles deep, according to the weather forecast? An unenviable situation in early November, yet it was a glimmer of hope to which we clung.

Water sloshing over the floorboards directed our attention to more immediate matters and we set to with panting determination. 'Well, there's no better bilge pump than a bucket and a scared man,' Chris quipped grimly. At a maddeningly slow pace we began to bale out the water, bucketful by bucketful. Slowly the water level inched downwards. The work was exhausting. I reached down, filled the bucket, then with deadening pain raised it to my shoulder where Chris, standing at the gaping hole that was once a sturdy hatch, emptied the contents overboard. Sometimes the bucket was jolted by the awkward motion of the half-submerged boat in the heavy seas, spilling the water back in.

The body felt no sudden shock of cold as the water poured over it. Nor did it feel pain as the knuckles repeatedly came into contact with hard surfaces. The only message was visual. A bright red flag of ragged skin and smudges of bloodstained water; strange. My tunnel vision of survival forced me to cancel out much of the information Chris's more encompassing mind had absorbed during our initial embrace. Gazing out over the foredeck, he had watched helplessly as compass, binnacle, depth sounder, engine controls and broken pieces of oak taffrail and doghouse, along with man-overboard gear, emergency flares, camera and precious film were consumed by the white foam as the waves broke around us. Unable to continue the hideous task of bailing for another moment, we would seek a brief respite by changing places. But the motion was relentless.

A steady rhythmic thud slowly penetrated our frozen minds.

What was it? Dulled curiosity stirred. As the water level began to drop, sensitivity to the noise grew. Unable to ignore it any longer, Chris went forward and, to his horror, discovered the cause. The force of the water had torn apart the dinghy chocks and washed the dinghy overboard. It remained attached to the boat with only a short length of rope. With each violent rise and fall of the hull, the alternately taut, then slack rope was causing the brass eyebolt on the bow of the dinghy to ram with fantastic force into the side porthole made of 13 mm (½ in) thick plate glass with a 30 cm (1 ft) diameter. It was only a matter of moments before the porthole gave way to the battering and shattered, as had the two ports in the aft cabin. The crucial difference was that this port was below the water line. If it broke, we would sink in a matter of moments. Crawling on all fours, Chris clawed his way to the foredeck to save the dinghy by pulling her on deck. I had stopped bailing in order to scrounge below for a knife which I found in a most unlikely place, the bathtub. In deadly earnest, yet at the same time feeling slightly ridiculous with a knife clenched between my teeth, I followed on hands and knees, making sure the safety harness was clipped on. Exposed to the full fury of the storm, Chris looked at me, took the knife and without a word, cut the dinghy free. It appeared that the force of the knockdown had split open the bottom of the fibreglass dinghy when it was lashed to the deck, upside down. It was useless and the sea quickly swallowed it up. *Laylah* was now our life raft.

The main and mizzenmasts of Douglas fir, cut from the forests of the Pacific north west and honed by Chris's hand, stood sturdy and erect, as did the standing rigging of galvanised iron, tied and carefully parcelled and served in the old traditional way. It is hard to say if the more modern but brittle stainless steel rigging would have withstood the same forces, for the rigging had stretched considerably, something stainless steel doesn't take to kindly. The gaff jaws had sheared off but the booms were sound — it was still a workable rig. The radar dome was swinging wildly, wrapped a dozen or so times around the mainmast it had tangled hopelessly in the rigging. Our tiny staysail, the only sail we had up at the time of the knockdown, was shredded beyond repair. What a sorry sight.

As we turned to go below, the furious wind whipped our faces. A distant shape appeared from nowhere. I strained hard to discern what it was. The now unmistakable grey silhouette of a freighter was pounding its way through the huge seas towards us. It must have picked up our Mayday. The cavalry had arrived, a marching band was playing. People, good cheer, dry clothes, laughter and companionship. I bathed in warm thoughts of rescue. Imperceptibly, without words, I could feel Chris hesitate. This would mean abandoning *Laylah* to the mercy of the seas. I sensed, and identified with, his intense struggle. Staring out across the sea, strewn with our debris as far as the eye could see in a long sad trail, it was hard to believe we had not already sunk. It also gave us time to appreciate the true scale of the seas that had been building around us over the past week. A series of storms and hurricanes had been brewing in the Kamchatka Peninsula. One freighter, we'd heard, had been lost off the coast of Japan with all hands on deck.

The weather had been unusual for the last year or so — probably the warming trend known as El Nino had something to do with it, causing warm seas to create extreme changes in the atmosphere. El Nino, the reversal of ocean currents, is a phenomenon caused by a reversal in atmospheric pressures between Indonesia and the south east Pacific. Generally, a strong El Nino brings the Atlantic fewer hurricanes and the Pacific more. The previous year the Pacific recorded 24 hurricanes, the greatest number on record. The large mass of ocean, unbroken by any land mass, gave plenty of time for the seas to build. We were being hit by fronts every 12 to 24 hours where literally the barometer would bottom out. Three days out of Kauai, part of the Hawaiian islands, we had hit our first gale that had blown us 260 km (160 miles) off course. This was the edge of a hole in hell into which we had dropped and now it appeared there was no getting out of it. Seventeen out of 21 days were recorded as gale force winds and above in our log.

Totally unaware that we were teetering on this brink, and busy with reefing the mainsail and changing the headsail, we inadvertently caught on our trailing fishing line a magnificent albatross with a wingspan of over 3 m (10 ft). It had been tracking our boat for days. Effortlessly riding on the thermal air currents while making very few wing flaps, it was capable of flying halfway round the world in a month. To see this creature being dragged along, skimming the wave tops with a large hook lodged in its gullet, was a painful sight. Due to its sheer weight we were unable to reel it in before the line broke, and we had to leave the poor bird tangled in the line while we sailed on. The weather had not let up for a minute, but the bird's inevitable death haunted me. At that moment I came to understand the superstitions of sailors of old.

'We've been saved.' Barely had the words passed my lips than ugly doubt nudged aside my short-lived joy when it became clear that waves were breaking over the housing of the large freighter. Spray carried clear over the cabin top and mast itself. It was obvious that any form of rescue, save that of a helicopter, would be suicidal. By now we were unable to establish radio contact with the captain. Saltwater in the electronics had taken its toll. The freighter lingered a safe distance off, long enough to ensure that we were remaining afloat, then gave a long, mournful signal and took off into the distant grey like a ghost ship in a dream.

Alone again, it was almost with relief that we returned to the task of bailing. The decision whether or not to abandon ship had been made for us. All three of us were in this together and we were

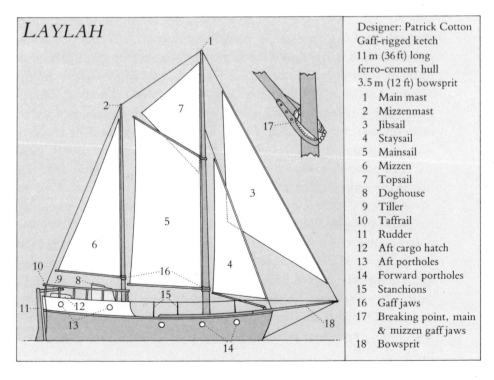

LAYLAH

Designer: Patrick Cotton
Gaff-rigged ketch
11 m (36 ft) long
ferro-cement hull
3.5 m (12 ft) bowsprit

1 Main mast
2 Mizzenmast
3 Jibsail
4 Staysail
5 Mainsail
6 Mizzen
7 Topsail
8 Doghouse
9 Tiller
10 Taffrail
11 Rudder
12 Aft cargo hatch
13 Aft portholes
14 Forward portholes
15 Stanchions
16 Gaff jaws
17 Breaking point, main & mizzen gaff jaws
18 Bowsprit

going to give it our best to get out of it. Self-reliance had always served us best in the mountains in the past. Once more it would be put to the test. As night fell and the water in the bilge became more manageable, we slowly began to put back the pieces of our shattered dream: to sail to Valdez, Alaska, and spend the winter ice-climbing in preparation for our winter climb of north face Kanchenjunga in the Himalayas. Delays in San Pedro, California, awaiting the completion — of all things — of light-weather sails, and then being held up in Kauai whilst a hurricane passed by, delayed our departure north until mid-October. We were unwilling to winter in Kauai and still held on to cherished thoughts of Alaska. The remoteness of its mountains, the chaotic abundance of its wildlife, the raging rivers and the moody ocean were a strong draw. In winter it was even more appealing. Now, all our energies were directed to reaching the mainland. To sail back into the full force of the storms to reach Kauai, although closer, was unrealistic. Better to run with the storms until we hit land. All thoughts of Alaska were abandoned.

In retrospect, our biggest mistake was having a fairly tight time schedule, and with sailing we were finding it can cause problems. Yet where does one draw that carefully defined line between persevering against high odds ultimately to succeed, and giving in to more conservative judgement? We had satisfying and demanding careers: Chris as a full-time physician in a busy inner-city emergency department in Los Angeles and myself as a registered nurse in an open-heart surgical unit. Putting the boat together for cruising acted as a balm, a total relief from the chaotic world of others' pain and suffering that was the normal part of our working life. To become totally absorbed in that day-to-day reality was easy. Mesmerised and deadened by the routine of existence, bolstered by the prestige that society places on a fat pay cheque, there was always some effort needed to break away. But we both understood the necessity of doing so. Juggling the organisation of the climbing and sailing preparation with long hours of non-synchronised work-shifts, was a lifestyle we had adapted to readily, but signs of stress were apparent. In addition, the syndrome of too much food, drink and good living had crept unwittingly into our lives. This was a purging.

My brother Pete came to visit us from the east coast. A long time sailor, Pete had built a steel Tasman seabird designed by Alan Payne, named *Scheherazade*, and sailed her round the world over the last ten years. We were eager to glean what we could from his years of experience. I remember so well in San Pedro, Pete sitting back in the aft cabin surveying the seaworthiness of our vessel. He had a good eye for such things, having been capsized and rolled over six times in 48 hours in the Tasman Sea off New Zealand. 'You are going to have to do something about this hatch, Cherie, better tie downs ... You know that if you take on a wave it will wipe the decks clean, it will take everything.' How true those words rang.

Somehow the detail of the hatch was put aside in hectic preparation. We were distracted by such things as installing radar to aid us with the difficult navigation of the coast of Alaska and preparing a 5 m (6 ft) diameter sea anchor that we planned to use in severe weather. Now the radar was gone and the sea anchor, which we had placed so much faith in after reading an article by the famed Larry Pardey, had proved somewhat of a disappointment. The size of the seas made heaving to impossible and the difficulty in actually employing the sea anchor in storm conditions with a two-person crew made its use impractical. Admittedly it gave us a few hours of respite, but inevitably the trip line became tangled and collapsed the sea anchor's shute and a line chafed through despite using preventive measures. And on inspection, the cloth in the shute was beginning to fail. We ended up using our anchor chain aft and trailing it, which did work, and we put the sea anchor aside for the ultimate storm, not knowing if we were already experiencing it.

At the time of our first knockdown we were running with the swells and steering with the small staysail. By morning, the furious wind of the previous night had dropped to about 40–45 knots, the sun had broken through and the barometer was rising. The boat was free of water and the portholes were sealed with heavy Gortex material stolen from our climbing supplies. The seas, however, were even more chaotic than the previous night. Encouraged by the drop in wind we brought in the drogues and started up the engine to see if it still worked after the saltwater immersion. It did. After the dark despair of the night, hope trickled through. With rays of sun to warm our souls, we got under way. Chris was scampering around with a big wrench tightening down all the turnbuckles and generally checking the rigging. I was at the helm fixed on keeping *Laylah*'s stern one quarter to the main swells. If this wasn't done, the boat was in danger of 'pitch-poling' or going bow-over stern in a big somersault which could cause extensive damage. It was a difficult job in such a sea, demanding constant attention due to the irregular spacing and direction of the swell.

Out of the corner of my eye a monster wave loomed. It was on us in a moment, swinging us high into the air. Clutching the tiller and the taffrail with all my might, I was overcome with a feeling of weightlessness. As the ship rolled I was plucked free. This was the very edge of life. There was nothing left to cling to. I sank into the water with a warm feeling, a final break from fatigue, tension and fear. Now I could rest.

The seaworthiness of the boat became apparent as she righted herself once more. A vast amount of water had again poured through the open hatches and portholes — the same scene as 24 hours previously. It was just too much, I couldn't believe it. Why hadn't we just sunk and got it over and done with, instead of suffering this slow torture? Chris, perched on the edge of the poop deck, had been thrown across and landed beside me. Both our safety harnesses had held, firmly attached to two tiedown points. This time Chris went below to clear up the mess while I continued at the helm into the night, until I dropped from exhaustion. Resigned to our fate, I tied off the tiller and went below. Chris had got the 12-volt bilge pump operating which spared us the gruelling work of hand bailing. We had immediately deployed the trailing ropes, called warps or drogues, which seemed to be working. The idea of using warps was to stop the vessel surging down the swells and turning or broaching sideways to the swell, increasing greatly the risk of capsize.

There remained the odious job of cleaning up. Anyone whose home has been ravaged by fire, flood or earthquake can identify with this heartbreaking task. A precious photo of family, carefully wiped clean and saved; favourite books found sodden and thrown overboard; clothes and down gear soaked and shoved into an unused corner; essential navigation tables, logs and charts carefully spread out in an attempt to dry them; usable food itemised and stowed, spoiled food thrown overboard. The ingredients of our survival slowly took shape. The fo'c's'le developed a womb-like atmosphere, a place where we could crawl to find, in the darkness and wet warmth of woollen blankets, some illusion of protection. Every so often an especially large cross swell would crash across the decks and shatter the veil of hard-won tranquillity. The feeling of impending doom with each of these violent intrusions caused — I imagined — a state not too different from that of a soldier on the front line in a state of shell shock. It fascinated me to observe these reactions as I had never imagined being held in the grip of such terror. A strong thread connected me to my two children, safely attending school on the other side of the world. I could hear my daughter Anna's voice screaming in my ear to hold on as her hand reached down to touch mine.

The following ten days are vague and ill-defined. Looking at the log the entrances are brief and taciturn, scrawled in a blunt pencil. 'Barometer dropped 13 points in two hours ... Drogues out ... Found small flints from lighter amongst tangle of fishing tackle and tools, able to light oil lantern ... Cleared carburettor from diesel stove today ... First hot meal in ten days ... Baked fresh bread, fresh water getting low, beginning to distil seawater. Weather pattern continues ... Weather map dotted with approaching gales and storms.'

I had thrown every conceivable sheet and towel onto the floor in order to help us stop sliding around so much on the slick oil-covered floor. It helped, but did not prevent Chris from being thrown violently across the galley into the stairwell, causing a few broken ribs. It was painful for him to breathe or haul on lines for the next week, and he was marked by an impressive bruise on his chest. An old knee injury of mine flared up making it twice the normal size. I hoped nothing more serious lay in store. We had jokingly referred to our uneventful sail from Los Angeles to Hawaii as the geriatric cruise. In retrospect it was developing all the qualities of Paradise, with memories of sitting out on deck under the fullness of the starry heavens, while *Laylah* coursed her way through the black waters breaking with phosphorescence.

On 26 November we hit a high pressure area and found ourselves becalmed. After days of gale and storm we sat out on deck in stunned silence under the blue sky while porpoises, as far as the eye could see, crested the waves in unison, four to six abreast. They had come together in their hundreds to celebrate the joy of life. Tears rolled down our cheeks as we unwittingly became participants. Not to be outdone, a school of 20–30 whales joined in the chorus. The water glistened and shone with shoals of swarming albacore. It was a magnificent display of nature's abundance.

As the sun set to a torrid red, the barometer began to fall. By 11 pm we had hove to once again. As we whittled away the kilometres towards land from 140° west to 130°, then down to 126° west longitude, we grew more cautiously optimistic. The AM/FM radio was picking up stations on the Washington and Oregon coast and we were able to hear the results of the gales we had experienced as they hit land. One hundred and forty-five kilometres an hour (90 mph) of wind in downtown Seattle, 95 km/h (60 mph) off the Oregon coast. 'I guess this isn't just one big hallucination,' we joked to one another. More importantly, the sound of human voices reaching out to us across the ocean became a powerful, magnetic attraction. For hours we would listen to dumb talk shows in which people would call up the DJ and shoot the breeze about sport, politics or some soap opera character. It was vital to keep up our spirits. Because much of our canned food had been lost through the open hatches, we were on survivial rations of only three glasses of water a day which we made into smoothies of powdered egg and milk with sugar, a caloric intake way below the energy we were using up. I could recognise a distinct improvement of morale as the blood sugar rose after we ate a can of tuna or fruit. We had both privately considered shooting ourselves to end the pain of existence — a thought not shared until months after the trip.

On the 39th day at sea, after heaving to the night before, we experienced moderate winds and a comfortable swell. We put out full sail and made excellent time for the next two days. At 0300 hours on 1 December, I first spotted Point Reyes lighthouse, north of San Francisco. By morning we were able to see land clearly. Drakes Bay lay on our portside and we impatiently took turns at staring through the binoculars at the wonderful sight of trees, grass and rolling hills. The smell of the earth filled our nostrils. We celebrated with a strawberry smoothie, the usual recipe with a prized can of strawberries thrown in. It was the last can from our supplies.

As our spirits rose the wind began to drop, little by little, until by four in the afternoon the sails were flapping listlessly. Becalmed at Point Bolinas, on the approach to San Francisco, without a functioning engine, we were at the mercy of the currents. We stood by helplessly as *Laylah* swung in circles with the changing flows. At one time we came to within half a kilometre of the rocks off Point Bonita and we stood by nervously, ready to drop the anchor at a moment's notice before being swept away by yet another current.

Laylah was now over the notorious Potato Patch Shoal. A semi-circular shoal with depths less than 11 m (36 ft), it is formed by silt deposits carried to the ocean by the Sacramento and San Joaquin river systems. Potato Patch Shoal and Four Fathoms Bank have reported depths of less than 7 m (23 ft). The name Potato Patch is said to have originated from the fact that schooners from Bodega Bay frequently lost their deckload of potatoes whilst crossing the shoal. Very dangerous conditions can develop whenever large swells generated by storms out at sea reach the shore; a natural condition called shoaling causes the large swells to amplify and increase in height when they move over shallow water shoals. (In fact, we were crossing a sea mount at the time of our knockdowns which indicates the changing character of the ocean.) This pulling up of water over the shoals is worsened when the tidal current is ebbing, that is, flowing out of the Golden Gate. The coastal pilot warns mariners to exercise extreme caution as conditions may change in a considerably short period of time. Waves short and steep, 6−7.5 m high (20−25 ft), have been reported capable of breaking a good ship apart. Perfectly calm, except for the peculiar sound of the waters rippling and quivering around us, with seemingly sinister intent, our instincts were alert to the potential danger. To make a landfall at night and enter a strange harbour without an adequate chart of the area is a sailing taboo. Better to heave to for the night and enter by good light, refreshed, the next day. The weather forecast on the radio was good, yet the sky was developing some disturbing mackerel clouds.

All reason was set aside, every muscle fibre, every cell in our body was reaching out to embrace land. There was no further debate, we would drift in through the Golden Gate Bridge with the tides, hoping the outgoing freighters would see us soon enough to take evasive measures. Sliding under the Gate in inky blackness, the lights of the commuting traffic flickered overhead — slaves of a separate reality.

A slight breeze picked up, just enough for us to feel our way towards the lights of San Francisco. The wind dropped once again, a mere 60 m (200 ft) from land. If only we had a dinghy we could have rowed over to a pier. Out of the darkness came the sound of a skiff and outboard, and noisy raucous laughter. 'Hey you guys, where can we tie up for the night, we're kind of tired and our diesel's out.' 'Have you got a rope — we'll take you to Fisherman's Wharf.' 'Sounds great.' In a flash the tow rope appeared and after a few false starts we made our way haphazardly to the dockside. We thanked our new friends profusely as other figures started appearing from nowhere, helping us with the docklines.

That task accomplished, the next essential thing was, where do we eat? Feeling our feet on solid ground for the first time in six weeks, we teetered over to Aliotos, a well known San Franciscan restaurant. Still in our sodden clothing, we were amused by the glances of the head waiter and the curious patrons. We did not care, we ate what we could but found our stomachs quite shrunken and our throats choked with emotion. The tastebuds did not flow freely. The sourdough bread and wine were much appreciated, but more than anything we enjoyed the warmth of the people around us. Our waiter even treated us to a bottle of wine.

Still in a state of shock, we walked back to the boat to find a handful of local fishermen coiling ropes and putting away gear and sails. 'Gee thanks, that's awfully nice of you.' 'Well, we figured anyone who pulls up in the middle of the night like that, ties up and walks off leaving things the way you did, has had one hell of a sail.' 'You can say that again mate. Want to come below and have a drink?' 'Mind if we bring some friends?' 'Hey, the more the merrier.' And so we partied and talked until dawn.

Some time in the early morning the wind started picking up. By seven o'clock it was blowing 45 knots and by ten o'clock the waves were breaking over the end of the dock. The Golden Gate Bridge was closed after a truck blew over. Winds measured 75 knots, and

120 knots on Mount Tamalpais. As we braced ourselves into the wind, walking down the street to call family and friends, Chris turned to me and said, 'So much for conventional wisdom as opposed to listening to the voice within. I hate to think where we'd be if we had waited until morning to come in.' 'Well we wouldn't be making this phone call, that's for sure,' I answered him with a hug.

And so one chapter closed and another one opened as we plunged into the life of San Francisco.

2

*He who sacrifices his conscience to ambition
Burns a picture to obtain the ashes.*

OLD CHINESE PROVERB

IT WAS IN many ways a tragedy that Chris and I were first to meet
in Pakistan, on the 1978 American K2 expedition. Both already in
committed relationships, over the ensuing four months we fell in
love. It was the beginning of a sequence of events that was to mark
a turning point in our lives forever.

I had heard that Chris was a doctor who was a very good
climber, wore his blond hair shoulder length, and in his spare time
was building a boat. I was fascinated and drawn by a compelling
desire to know him better. We were introduced by Jim Whittaker,
the expedition leader, in the oppressive heat of Pakistan's Rawalpin-
di airport. Offering me his upturned thumb with mocked seriousness, Chris said, 'Would you mind putting your index finger here
please.' I did so, obligingly. A loud fart echoed forth. I blushed
awkwardly, embarrassed, not knowing quite what to do next. Our
eyes met, and recognising I'd been caught off guard, we both
laughed uproariously at the joke. He was a man who had no time
for the pretences of society. I warmed to him immediately.

Chris was born in the Pacific north west of America. The Cas-
cade Mountains were a natural school and playground for him
where he developed his skills as a climber and skier. He was the
first man to ski down Mount McKinley, in Alaska, after which he
took several trips to the Andes and finally the Himalayas, reaching
the summit of Mount Everest in 1976. He casually brushed aside his
disarming good looks and academic brilliance with a candour that I
suspect was designed to diffuse the jealousy and competitiveness he
sometimes aroused in those less talented.

This was my first experience of a large expedition and I felt awkward and overwhelmed by the number and diversity of people with whom I was to eat, sleep and climb over the next four months. My previous climbing experience, even on extended expeditions to remote areas in the Himalayas, had always been an intimate two-to-four person venture. I felt more comfortable about facing the challenge that the mountain presented than I did about fitting into the social hierarchy of our team. To be part of a group of like-minded individuals bonded with a strong sense of teamwork is ideal. Each team member selflessly gives up his own unspoken but cherished desires for the summit in favour of the ultimate success of the expedition as a whole. This model can be discussed, idealised and desired most sincerely, but to achieve it in reality may be even more elusive than the summit itself.

A team of three doctors — Rob Schaller, Skip Edmunds and Chris Chandler; a registered nurse — myself; a neurobiologist — Lou Reichardt; a nuclear physicist — Bill Sumner, who built and designed outdoor equipment; an anthropologist — Terry Bech (my husband); a lawyer — Jim Wickwire, known as 'Wick'; an author and self-described shipwright — Rick Ridgeway; and a zoologist — Craig Anderson teamed up with a professional climber — John Roskelley; an outdoor equipment salesperson — Diana Jagerský; a professional photographer — Dianne Roberts and her husband — expedition leader Jim Whittaker. We were a mixed bag of well qualified people. Our climbing backgrounds had an equal measure of variety, versatility and talent and we had every chance of success. Yet chastened by personal experience or sobered by tales of other large expeditions and their pitfalls, it was commonly agreed that our experience would be different.

We set out in the manner and style of old British attempts on Everest — to conquer the mountain. Or, as put more succinctly by the leader, 'to knock the bastard off' — an attitude I found rather distasteful. There was no talk of probing investigation to establish a rapport with the mountain to see what she might give us in return. For those who have not experienced the feeling, it probably hovers dangerously in the realm of the supernatural. For others more comfortable with such things, one is 'in tune' with the mountain and often tempted to give it human or godlike traits. Perhaps much of this is transference of one's own fears, doubts and desires, something that is easily done when in daily, intimate contact with the mountain, deprived of any or few outside influences for months at a time.

Descending Dhaulagiri with Terry, in spring 1971, in the wake of an early monsoon beset with heavy, wet snow avalanches and gaping, wide crevasses that blocked our escape, thoughts such as these entered my mind. In the wake of one such avalanche my Aussie digger hat blew off with the accompanying gust of wind. We had descended the final snow gully that led to the base of the mountain and safety was ours. However, the hat landed about 30 m (100 ft) away at the foot of a serac, a tall pinnacle of ice. I hesitated, torn between the luxurious feeling of being finally off the mountain and wanting to fetch my favourite hat. The sense of being regurgitated from the very bowels of the mountain overcame me. Moments later, the ice tower collapsed. Tons of ice buried my hat forever and would have buried me too had I not listened to the mountain.

Earlier in the Dhaulagiri trip there were instances such as me saying, 'Gee, I wish we had some salt — we're just about out.' I looked down at my feet and there in the snow lay a small bag of salt left over from a previous expedition. I laughed. It's not that the presence or absence of salt had any real effect on the outcome of the climb, it's just that the incident, along with others on the trip, produced an uncanny feeling.

Mallory stated when he looked at Everest, 'What have we come to conquer? Only ourselves.' In the most esoteric sense I believed the mountain gave us every opportunity to do just that, providing the mirror through which we could view ourselves. It was up to us to deal with it as best we could. In that sense, the mountain is every bit human and godlike. On the K2 expedition the dominant personalities of the key team members, which set the tone of the expedition, did not appear to share this view. There was also the problem that media exposure and publicity were crucial to the success of raising a $100,000 budget from various outdoor equipment specialists and, if lucky, *National Geographic* magazine. This probably contributed to the group assuming the role of conquerer and adopting a language that the advertising world and general public could relate to easily.

The official account of the expedition has already been told by Ridgeway in *The Last Step*. I shall not pretend here to reveal the entire story but will merely present my own narrow perspective of a very personal encounter with a group of people, each of whom bear their own scars of the experience.

The decision to go on a major climb usually forces a climber to step back and consider some pretty hard questions: What am I doing with my life? Is this really where I want to be in the greater plan of things? Philosophical questions aside, the professional, financial and personal consequences of taking off four months can be considerable, possibly devastating, and as the mother of two children, the questions are even more poignant. Even so, when considering the pros and cons, I found myself more often than not back in the mountains where I could gain a perspective so easily clouded by the clamorous noise of daily existence. Returning five months pregnant from a photographic reconaissance of the north east spur of Dhaulagiri, seven years before, brought stern frowns of disapproval from other climbers, friends and acquaintances at a time when cigarette smoking and drinking alcohol during pregnancy barely raised an eyebrow. It was an unpopular choice to be a serious climbing mother, and I was putting on the line the bond of love that joined me to my children, trusting that our common love would carry us through the pain caused by separation. With a solemn face my son Daniel, then four years old, counselled me to carry a parachute at all times lest I should fall and the rope break. He had heard K2 was the second highest mountain in the world and very steep.

So, with a willingness to accept pain in return for growth, I exchanged a more comfortable role in the All Women's American Annapurna Expedition in Nepal for the challenge of a country I had never visited. I joined an exclusively male team, except for the leader's wife Dianne Roberts as expedition photographer and Diana Jagerský as Base Camp manager.

A recurring nightmare before the trip puzzled me: I was pursued, captured and raped by a marauding band of men grown into monsters. The tops of their heads were sawn open and the brains scooped out. The real horror came when they bent down to rape me repeatedly, forcing me to look into their cavernous skulls. They thought themselves beautiful, and raping me was their method of attempting to convince me to be the same as them. As the expedition rolled on, the dream kept coming back to me.

Ambition, says B.C. Forbes, is the mainspring of nearly all progress, yet uncontrolled and unbridled it can spur people into cruel and despicable deeds. Without ambition we are morally dead, but supreme care must be taken that it does not kill us spiritually. Ambition may be likened to a spirited horse — it can carry us quickly over much ground if we keep a proper rein on it and guide it along the right road. Given too much rein it could land us in a ditch. The 1978 American K2 expedition landed in a ditch.

I understood a certain amount of alienation was the result of my liaison with Chris; it is human nature to take sides in such affairs and I was definitely the 'bad guy'. But I sensed an alienation that went deeper. For all the talk of enlightened attitudes of the 1980s and the equality of women, sociological studies show that successful men still admit to prejudice against their female counterparts who operate on the same level of competency. This attitude saddened me. I wasn't there to prove my muscles were as big as theirs — a ten-second arm wrestling match would have ended that debate. To be accepted and appreciated for what I could contribute would have been enough. The strength of a butterfly does not appear very

ABOVE: *Since early times, nature and the earth have been linked with women and seen as a kind and nurturing mother as well as a wild and uncontrollable female. When the view swung to wild and uncontrollable it gave rise to the need to dominate nature. The widely used terms among mountain climbers such as 'conquer' and 'assault' reflect this thinking. (Photo Chris Chandler)*

BELOW: *Porters in the monsoon rain on approach march to Everest. The exploitation of nature has gone hand in hand with the exploitation of women. It is not an uncommon sight to see between 300 and 1,000 porters moving through a fragile mountain environment like a plague of locusts, stripping the countryside bare of human resources, food and firewood. (Photo Chris Chandler)*

OVERLEAF: *Following the tactics of an army doing battle, part of the logistics of the assault include large quantities of oxygen, fixed line and lots of people. For Sherpas, whose income may depend on this kind of work, it extracts a horrible death toll. Here, the leader of the K2 Expedition, Jim Whittaker, is greeted by Chris with a welcome cup of tea after a strenuous load carry to Camp 2. (Photo Dianne Roberts)*

formidable, yet a butterfly has the capacity to migrate thousands of miles. The power I sensed within me was not brute strength but an enduring affinity with the spirit that moves a butterfly.

The expedition philosophy might have been more properly revealed at the outset as 'A certain number of you are chosen for the summit, the remaining members are here to carry loads.' This would have relieved the problem of false expectations, and given potential members a choice as to whether they wished to participate or not under such circumstances. Considering the personal and financial sacrifices that such an expedition demands, this would have seemed only fair. Instead, everyone was encouraged actively to believe that we all started out with a chance of reaching the summit.

The chosen summit members, however, were Rick Ridgeway, John Roskelley, Lou Reichardt and Jim Wickwire. These four were endorsed by the leader as the strongest and best climbers and those most likely to succeed. We were disgruntled and unhappy that we had been eliminated so early in the trip from even a striking chance at the summit. We called them the A Team, and mollified ourselves with the label B Team for 'best'. We each adopted our roles and acted out the melodrama more befitting an opera by Puccini than K2 by the Americans. As it happened, there was an unprecedented seven-day stretch of perfect weather which could have allowed the entire team to reach the summit.

To alleviate our frustration at not being able to fly free and feel the creative flow of energy that the mountains usually bring, the B Team presented a plan for consideration. This was to launch a simultaneous summit attempt. The A Team would continue from Camp 5, along the direct finish via the north east ridge — the so-called Polish route. The remainder of the B team who felt fit enough would attempt the Abruzzi Ridge — not as technical but

LEFT: *Climbers ferrying loads between Camps 3 and 4 on the Polish route, K2. (Photo John Roskelley)*

PREVIOUS PAGE ABOVE: *The western cwm on Mount Everest dwarfs man's ambitions. (Photo Chris Chandler)*

PREVIOUS PAGE BELOW: *High camp, Mount Everest. Kanchenjunga can be seen, shimmering like a Polynesian island in a sea of cloud, nearly 160 km (100 miles) to the east on the far left horizon. (Photo Chris Chandler)*

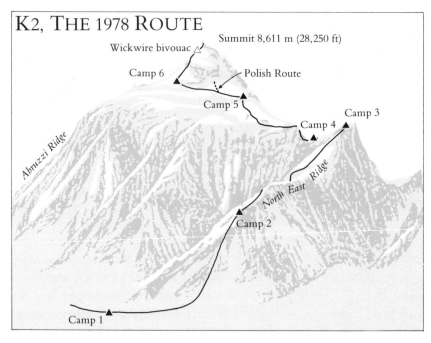

K2, THE 1978 ROUTE

Summit 8,611 m (28,250 ft)

Wickwire bivouac

Camp 6

Polish Route

Camp 5

Camp 3

Camp 4

Abruzzi Ridge

North East Ridge

Camp 2

Camp 1

demanding nonetheless — in modified Alpine style, that is without fixed lines. Not only did it give more people a chance to go for the summit, but it increased back-up support for the direct finish team and improved the chances of putting someone on the top.

A charge of energy passed through the battered morale of the B Team at the thought of it. To our surprise, after very little discussion, the A Team accepted the plan. That night we stood around Base Camp in a circle of prayer, while John Roskelley and Rick Ridgeway sat out at Camp 4, reluctant to return to Base Camp for fear a break in the weather would occur and precious time be lost returning to their present altitude and lead position. Jim Whittaker spoke of brotherhood and sisterhood, our united purpose and asked for God's blessing on us all. Later that night, Lou Reichardt secured from Chris the only oxygen bottle wrench used to break open the seal before the cylinder can be used. As medical officer in charge of the oxygen, Chris was reluctant to part with this precious tool for fear it would be lost or misplaced, but Reichardt said that he personally wanted to check the equipment.

With the rest of the B Team, as a show of gratitude, I had agreed to make one more carry to Camp 5 to ensure the success of the A

Team. Lists were compiled — everybody knew precisely what they were to carry and what essential items were to be picked up for each camp along the designated route. We were scheduled to leave at predetermined times in the morning to avoid traffic jams on the fixed lines, and Chris and I were to be the first to leave. When we awoke we found a deserted camp. The A Team had already headed off up the mountain. Terry Bech, Skip Edmunds and Bill Sumner were as puzzled as Chris and I. On reaching Camp 2, none of the items we were supposed to pick up were there, including some things deemed essential by the B Team to succeed on the alternative route, such as extra stoves and gas cartridges.

Jim Whittaker and Dianne Roberts were lagging behind and we could see them disappearing in rapidly deteriorating weather along the ridge that separated Camps 3 and 4. Communicating with John Roskelley on the two-way radio confirmed that concern for Jim and Dianne's safety was felt by all. We were about to set out to look for them when they finally arrived by flashlight at Camp 4, cold and very tired.

The next day dawned bright and clear, yet our orders were not to move another step higher on the mountain. Jim and Dianne needed a rest day. A black cloud hung over Chris, who resigned from further participation and descended to Base Camp in stony silence. As much as I was depressed by the situation, I wasn't ready to turn my back on the mountain. I couldn't find it in myself to do so. The sun shone too brightly, the sky was too outrageously blue. This meant a reunion of sorts with Terry who, since my relationship with Chris, had kept up a stoic front. Now we were on a rope together again. If our marriage were to survive this would be the test. Yet it was already too far gone. Smothered resentment and hostility loomed, suppressed rage was kept in tight check. Terry moved excessively slowly. So slowly, I had to wait over two hours for him at the end of fixed lines, getting very chilled in the process. Acutely aware of the delicate situation between us, I said nothing and we continued at a snail's pace to Camp 5, arriving well after dark. I was verging on hypothermia and John Roskelley reported to Base Camp via radio that I was mumbling and incoherent.

I was so relieved to be in camp and find warmth from sleeping bags, warmed bodies and hot drinks. My hands were still very cold and I asked Lou, who was lying next to me, if I could warm them on his stomach. He agreed, but when I tried to get close he gave a convulsive reaction and put my hands on his chest. I giggled to myself at the imagined newspaper headline: CRAZED WOMAN RAPES DEFENCELESS MAN AT 7,700 METRES.

The next morning I roped up with Lou Reichardt and Jim Wickwire and we started out for Camp 6. My hands were beginning to freeze up again and I wanted to adjust my gloves, but as Lou was jerking impatiently on the rope, all I could do was stumble along as best I could. I faced the biting cold of the vast snow plateau at 7,700 m (25,500 ft) and imagined I could see Chris's figure standing there bathed in the soft golden light of early morning. An impish smile played across his lips and a shine in his eyes blended with a diamond glint of snow. My heart ached to be with him. The time had come for me to turn around. The vision of Chris standing there and the feelings we had shared together on the mountain stood out in stark contrast to my present companions with whom I shared nothing. I unroped and walked back to camp alone.

I lay back in the relative luxury of a sleeping bag in a roomy tent and looked out over the clouds as though I was seated in a jet plane waiting for the stewardess to bring some coffee. Alone for the first time in months, I let my mind wander. Terry's return from Camp 6 broke a solitary vigil and we both descended to Camp 3 and waited. Twice Terry had carried loads for Roskelley and Reichardt to enable them to make the final summit bids on a 7,800 m (26,000 ft) peak. The first had been on Dhaulagiri in 1973.

Meanwhile, the real drama was going on above us. In the period of time that I had spent in close quarters with the A Team, sharing their tent and meals, endless discussions had taken place as to who would rope up with whom. A philosophy of 'every man for himself' was articulated and it was commonly agreed that each member had a greater or 'higher' individual responsibility to his family at home than to his climbing partner. These conversations astonished me because I believe the symbolic rope, the bond that joins two people, is unique to climbing for it literally places each person's life in the hands of another. This physical and spiritual bond is part of the magic of climbing, a magic so real that even when the rope is removed, the bond can remain.

On K2 in 1953 a different group of Americans was huddled together, immobilised for ten days in a storm. One of the climbers, Art Gilkey, developed blood clots in his legs and then his lungs, which often accompanies long periods of inactivity and dehydration at high altitude. What followed is remembered as one of the finest examples of climbing tradition. An epic descent, lowering down a critically ill man on an improvised stretcher, and a fall in which the lives of six were saved miraculously by the ice axe belay of the seventh. Gilkey was later swept away in an avalanche, probably saving the lives of his would-be rescuers. The question of leaving him behind was never considered — are such heroics merely old-fashioned ideas of a different era?

Charles Houston MD, in his eloquent article about climbing ethics in American Alpine Journal Vol. 27, poses such a question. He discusses a number of incidents that highlight the issues involved: the pressure of competition, the quest for fame and fortune along with the human need to reach out beyond one's limits, and a burning need to be counted by the highest ethical code of conduct. He describes an incident on Chogolisa in Concordia, Pakistan, in 1980. Two climbers were swept almost 900 m (3,000 ft) down the mountain by an avalanche. The third member of the team, climbing down, found them alive but too injured to move. There was a Japanese party high on the same mountain ready to make a summit bid. The third climber was able to contact them by radio. They responded immediately, giving up all chances of reaching the summit to evacuate the injured men, who were still alive after five days.

Climbing history abounds with similar instances of such selflessness. A fine line is drawn, however, between how far one goes to save the life of another, before directing that energy to save one's own life. How great is the moral obligation of one person to another. What if it were foolish even to try, or the climber had been warned not to go? The 1971 International Expedition, when four eminent climbers in near blizzard conditions were finally forced to admit defeat in rescuing Bahuguna, an Indian climber, is another example of such painful choices. It must have been a terrible decision to descend, leaving the poor man frostbitten, exposed and near death.

Houston warns us to be very careful not to fault a climber for

Based on observations by various Karakorum. Hindu-Kush expeditions and the map by the Survey of India. All altitudes are in metres. [©1978 Tsuneo MIYAMORI]

being self serving when danger is a constant threat and higher faculties have been blunted by oxygen deprivation. It is all too easy from the warmth of a cosy fireside to be critical about such actions. Judging by the furore the press created over the incident, implying the climbers callously left the man behind to die, shows it clearly had no idea of the reality of the situation.

Lou Reichardt and Jim Wickwire stood on the summit of K2. Lou took a few minutes for the obligatory record photograph of the event and descended alone without waiting for Jim, who wandered around in the oxygen-thin air for 35 minutes, taking in the scenery. He managed to make it down 100 m (328 ft) or so before realising it was very late. He was forced to bivouac out at 8,500 m (28,000 ft) without the down jacket and bivouac sack that he had had to leave behind. His only means of warmth was a pair of down pants I gave him before he left to make the summit bid.

There is something very sinister in melting snow at extreme altitudes. Not only does it rob the air surrounding the stove of oxygen but it produces a lethal carbon monoxide. Terry commented that a momentary loss of consciousness may have caused Wick to spill the liquid, resulting in further melting of snow the night before the summit attempt. A vicious circle is produced, but what choices are available when one knows how crucial it is to rehydrate oneself? It helps to recognise that it is not simple clumsiness, and to share the task of melting the snow, if at all possible, in such cramped conditions. Whatever the reason, Wick was without down jacket or bivvy sac during the ordeal of preventing himself from sliding off his narrow platform. He was becoming increasingly hypothermic, dehydrated and weak from lack of oxygen. The risk of frostbite was critical at one third atmospheric pressure.

With the intensity and focus of an initiated yogi, Wick's loved ones became the candle to which he was drawn, warmed by and led so gently back to the world of the living. Barely able to move his stiffened body, he continued to descend in the morning. He crossed

ABOVE: *Neither desert heat nor arctic cold can deter these porters wishing to carry to the base of K2. (Photo Chris Chandler)*

BELOW: *Chris, with a drained expression, rests inside the tent. He is on the south col of Everest on his return from the summit. (Photo Mike Hoover)*

paths with Roskelley and Ridgeway who were carrying two full bottles of oxygen for the summit bid. Ironically, they climbed on a few more minutes and then decided to jettison the cylinders with thoughts of a record-making oxygenless descent in mind. The precious gas that Wick so badly needed sat uselessly in the snow.

Aware only by radio that the summit was reached, Terry and I, waiting as support team at Camp 3, watched as the small black dots in the snow descended. One, two, three, four, everybody accounted for. We scurried around anticipating their arrival with gallons of melted water. Wick stuck his head through the Camp 3 tent door. In stark contrast to the others' deep tans his face was deathly pale, his respiration shallow and he was barely able to talk. He complained of sharp pains in his chest as though he had a broken rib. Later, this was diagnosed as blood clots in the lung and pneumonia.

The weather had turned and we were stormbound for several days. The rest of the expedition was packed up and ready to leave the mountain. A strange feeling of isolation crept in. Voices on the two-way radio demanded that we leave immediately and come down in a snowstorm; the same voices that had ordered Chris and I to carry loads over avalanche-prone slopes weeks earlier. I had always questioned the supposed 'safety in numbers' theory of a large expedition. What help were they to us there at 7,000 m (23,000 ft). I began to question it even more. The crack that had developed in the myth of the safety of a large expedition widened even further.

Finally the storm broke and we moved down to Base Camp. Rob Schaller appeared from his tent to examine the ailing Wick. I offered to set up some oxygen for him. 'Cherie, he doesn't need oxygen, what he really needs is to get to a lower elevation.' Afraid that a personality clash would further interfere with Wick's care, Chris and I withdrew totally. A helicopter mercifully plucked Wick

Kanchenjunga main summit. 'The whole north face of the mountain might be imagined to be constructed by the demon of Kanchenjunga for the express purpose of defence against human assault. So skilfully is each comparatively weak spot raked by the ice and snow batteries, I failed to see any route on which skill could avoid these difficulties.' Douglas Freshfield, 1899

off the glacier and away to civilisation and appropriate medical management.

At the bottom of the mountain the mighty Baltoro River had fallen probably 15 m (50 ft) or more while we had been on the mountain. On the walk back, a rope bridge was constructed in order to cross one of the Baltoro's tributaries safely — the Dumor-do. We elected to link arms and cross in groups of four or six. The water was at thigh-level and on the borderline of safety. The current was so swift and cold that only seconds after being immersed, all sensation was lost in the lower extremities. Terry chose to link arms with some porters who looked about half his size. With legs like spindles they succumbed to the cold immediately. Terry stepped on a boulder, it rolled, he lost his footing and started to topple. The tiny porters were unable to support him. A bulky pack compounded the problem. The river saw its victim and snapped its jaws around him. We all stood and stared in disbelief as the river swept Terry away at a frightening pace. Only Chris moved. Skipping agilely over the boulder-strewn shore, with an eye marked to where the current would bring him closer to the shore's edge, Chris waded in up to his waist and grabbed Terry. Nearby, porters were quick to retrieve Terry's pack and assist Chris. I suppose that this is one of the reasons my kids liked Chris so much. He had saved their father's life without thought of his own safety.

And so the expedition hobbled the 160 km (100 miles) out to Skardu on frost-damaged feet, swollen painfully in the desert sun. Shadowy ghosts of the robust team we had once been. With nothing but each other and a handful of ashes for the picture we so desired, Chris and I turned our backs on the large expedition forever.

3

*T*he self-contained man scorns help gained in
a dubious fashion. He thinks it more graceful
to go on foot than to drive in a carriage under false
pretences.

I   CHING

FALLING into a crevasse on K2 was a lesson I needed to learn about
life rather than about climbing out of a crevasse. It showed me how
easily a woman, conditioned by a conventional role, falls into a
pattern of following orders given by a man, and succumbs to male
authority and judgement. Foolishly thinking I was being regarded
as an equal, I didn't dream I had to prove myself in the crevasse
incident, and made the mistake of accepting help from people who
proved to be far from friendly.

I fell in as a number of people had done that sunny morning
walking up the glacier from Camp 1. My pack was hauled out
efficiently. As I cleaned the snow from around my neck and shoulders and fixed assenders and slings to the rope, people congregated
around the hole above me, peering down to see if I was OK.
Roskelley barked out to me, 'Clip onto the second rope, Cherie,' as
it was lowered down. 'It will be safer.' In the annoying way that
society has successfully trained women I obligingly followed his
orders. No sooner had I done so than the snow bridge I was
standing on collapsed and I fell down several more feet. I found
myself now in a bell-shaped cavern spinning around helplessly, the
two ropes twisting around one another. As I was unable to fix
myself to the walls of the crevasse, I waited patiently for the ropes
to untwine. The babble above had reached a crescendo. When the
offer came to haul me out I accepted lightheartedly, not giving a
second thought to the consequences. With three or four strong men
hauling on the line I was out in a matter of moments. This is in
fact, on large expeditions, a very common way of extricating

people from holes. The style of mountaineering I was accustomed to had made me, as a matter of course, self-reliant; often the only form of rescue was self-rescue. Never did I envisage that my accepting help in this situation would cancel me out as a competent climber on the first day of the expedition. Chris's climbing skills had been similarly maligned on the 'first step' of the route to Camp 2.

Chris was a nurturer with inexhaustible gentle energy devoted to developing his own skills and the skills of those who sought him out. He was a natural teacher and healer, not only of physical maladies, but those of the spirit too. He was good to be around and gave much just by his physical presence. A shining light towards which people were drawn. He supported my own instinctive desires to reach out and seek my limits without hint of competition. The problems I had encountered with the male climbers on K2 never interfered with my climbing relationship with Chris.

With that familiar mix of dread and bounding excitement that precedes a Himalayan climb, we set about planning our little trip to the north face of Yalung Kang, Kanchenjunga's western summit, 8,505 m (27,903 ft), in the spring of 1981. A necessary purging of all the garbage that we still carried with us from the K2 experience.

Kanchenjunga is the third highest mountain in the world. At 8,586 m (28,168 ft) it stands a scant 25 m (85 ft) lower than K2, some 1,500 km (900 miles) away in Pakistan. Seen above Darjeeling many people thought Kanchenjunga was the world's highest, in part because this spectacular massif has five major summits, four of which are above 7,800 m (26,000 ft), and in part because it is so easily viewed by city folk in the dusty, noisy streets of Darjeeling as an unending source of inspiration and beauty. The name Kanchenjunga translates as 'five treasure houses in the snow'. In Tibetan mythology it is believed that the five summits were store houses for the Goddess's treasures. The peak which most conspicuously reflected the rising sun stored gold; the peak which cast deep, cold grey shadows stored silver. The remaining peaks held copper, corn and sacred books.

Some 70 km (45 miles) to the north of Darjeeling and 130 km (80 miles) east of Everest, Kanchenjunga lies on the border of Sikkim and Nepal. The main north-south ridges of the mountain form a natural boundary between the two countries as well as a watershed between the Teesta and Kosi river systems. Lying about 20 km (12 miles) south of the main Himalayan chain, it sits alone and receives the first and heaviest precipitation from the monsoons, travelling fresh from the Bay of Bengal.

The result is a mountaineer's nightmare of hanging glaciers and ice cliffs. Douglas Freshfield in his trip around Kanchenjunga in 1899 wrote of the north face: 'The whole north face of the mountain might be imagined to be constructed by the demon of Kanchenjunga for the express purpose of defence against human assault. So skilfully is each comparatively weak spot raked by the ice and snow batteries, I failed to see any route on which skill could avoid these difficulties.'

It is not surprising that by 1977 only six mountaineers had reached its main summit from the south, that is, leaving the last few feet of the summit untrodden to respect the sanctity of the mountain. The lamas of Sikkim claimed that the 1977 Indian expedition had disturbed the Goddess even on the approach march. A loud explosion, followed by avalanches and mud slides, killed thousands of fish in the glacial streams. An expedition member was later killed in an icefall. These two expeditions were both large, using oxygen and numerous porters.

An essential element of our trip was to have a close communion between the climbers, most easily achieved by restricting the numbers to just the two of us. It automatically followed that we would climb in lightweight Alpine style, using a minimum of fixed lines. Freed from the competitiveness that can lead to rash decisions which we had experienced in the past, this would be truly 'our' trip. Decisions could be totally our own which was important as we could be dealing with life and death issues. Unaffected by radio calls from Base Camp or the considerations of possibly an unwieldy film crew, we would have free head space. Without oxygen we would not require high altitude porters or fellow climbers to risk their lives unnecessarily with repeated load carries up avalanche-prone slopes. We would be truly free to climb to our limits, using all the combined Himalayan experience we possessed, in a way simply not possible on a large expedition.

As only the fourth climbing party in 100 years to the north face we intended to make as little impact as possible on the fragile Alpine environment; we elected ourselves to be examples of 'how it should be done'. The first attempt was made by Norman Dyhrenfurth in 1930. This expedition was abandoned after a high altitude porter was killed climbing the first ice cliff. The second attempt from the north was in 1979 by Doug Scott's four-man team, three of whom successfully reached the summit via the north col, without the use of oxygen. Tragically, Pete Boardman, Joe Tasker and Georges Brettenbourg have since been killed on other mountains. A grim reminder — as if one is needed — of the weight carried by the decision to climb. The Japanese, with a 15-member team, a full contingent of Sherpas and 3,000 m (10,000 ft) of fixed line, climbed the north face with classic 'siege type' tactics. They placed two members on top. However, no attempt had been made from the north on Yalung Kang.

Yalung Kang had been climbed from the south, possibly as many as three times. The Kyoto University Academic Alpine Club expedition placed Takeo Masuda and Yutaka Ageta on the summit on 14 May 1973. Tragically, Yutaka was unable to proceed down after a bivouac at 8,000 m (27,000 ft) and when Takeo descended he was hit by a rock and fell to his death. In 1975 an 11-member Austrian-German Expedition led by Aberli put nine members on the summit, including one woman. They used oxygen for the last 600 m (2,000 ft). A third attempt was made in 1980 by a group of Mexicans via the Austrian-German route. But again the summit day resulted in disaster. The two summiteers, using oxygen, probably reached the summit but were never heard of again.

The I Ching cautioned us to exercise the skill and cunning of an old fox crossing a frozen lake. A younger, less experienced fox, seeing the distant shore coming within easy reach, breaks his concentration. At that very moment, the ice cracks open and he suffers the indignity of getting his tail wet. All the care he had exercised to get to his present position is wasted in a single careless move. Unfortunately we had much more to lose than the minor indignity of a wet tail. Nonetheless, we felt secure that given the right mental attitude based on humility, and wanting to do no harm to our fellow creatures or environment, we would be OK.

On 3 March 1981, elated at being treated as trekkers by the

Nepalese customs officials so that the usually heavy tariffs and import duties were waived, we entered Kathmandu. The climbing capital of the world, it boasts close to 200 expeditions per year. Countless tourists desiring to trek through the foothills and obtain first-class views of the Himalayan giants have added a confusion and commercialism that was scarcely noticeable ten years earlier.

Legend tells, substantiated by geological data, that the Kingdom of Nepal (known now as Kathmandu) was once a lake surrounded by snow-clad mountains. According to ancient texts, Stella Kramrisch writes, no man could approach this lake. A Buddha from a former aeon, focusing on the destiny of Nepal, threw a lotus seed into its waters. A miraculous lotus arose and bloomed in the middle of the lake. A flame, purer and more splendid that the rays of the sun, shot up from its centre. This is how the Adi Buddha, the Buddha from before all time, was manifested directly in his essence. Manjusri left his home in far-away China and with a sword 'moon smile' he cut through the mountains, cleaving a gorge through the rocks, known as Pharping Gorge in the Maharbharat Range.

The Bhagmati River now drains the fertile green valley. Years earlier I had lived on Chobar, a hill situated immediately over the gorge. I was engulfed in memories of a past life, living in a small valley, 1,350 m (4,500 ft) above sea level, 29 km (18 miles) long from east to west and 19 km (12 miles) wide north to south. Its people are Newars, related to other Mongoloid people of the entire country of Nepal, and form the bulk of the ancient inhabitants of the valley.

It is they who created the art of Nepal, preserving traditions with India whilst developing their own distinctive language, music and architecture. Tradition speaks of a long association with India, Tibet and China. The vast Himalayan chain and lack of roads appears to have posed no particular barrier to communication and the exchange not only of goods such as soft pashima blankets and salt but also the prized workmanship of Nepalese artists, who were recognised and recorded for their skill and facility as early as the seventh century. Mary Slusser, Nepalese art expert, claims the pagoda, the familiar design of temples, shrines and dwellings, found its birthplace in Kathmandu. It was inspired by the distinctive peak of Langtang (2,208 m/7,245 ft), seen from the valley floor

KANCHENJUNGA AND ITS WESTERN PARTS

Based on observations by various Himalayan expeditions and the maps by the Survey of India. All altitudes are in metres. [©1977 Yoshimi YAKUSHI]

as the highest peak of the Langtang Himal directly north of Kathmandu. The sides of its symmetrical slopes coincide precisely with the angle of a pagoda roof.

For all the thick suffocation of diesel fumes belching forth from lorries and buses clogging the narrow streets, and the shop merchants' guile at getting the best of a bargain with a *kuere*, or 'white monkey', we had undoubtedly returned to a magical kingdom, devoid of foreign influence as little as 30 years earlier. Now the present King Birendra Bir Bickram Shah Deve, the Living Incarnate of Lord Vishnu himself, was pressed to make up for lost time. Tourism was seen as an obvious and readily available source of foreign exchange. Unhappily, the impact of visitors to Sagarmatha National Park alone has been of alarming severity and serves as a painful illustration of how the remainder of the country could suffer.

Tourism began in the Khumbu region that forms the Sagarmatha National Park (around the base of Mt Everest) in the early 1950s, and by 1982 more than 5,000 visitors had entered the park. It was reported that tourism revenue rose from near zero in 1961 to 2.2 million rupees in 1971 and to 52 million rupees in 1981. On the plus side, the trickle-down effect considerably increased the income of the Khumbu residents, replacing the income once earned from trading with Tibet. However, with half the Khumbu forests missing in the decade ending in 1975, the heyday would soon be over.

In 1980 the National Parks and Wildlife Conservation banned the sale of firewood to trekking groups and expeditions, and the burning of outdoor fires in all the high altitude national parks. Trekkers must now take sufficient quantities of kerosene for cooking and washing. B.A. Coburn, Unesco consultant, points out, however, that many do not comply with outdoor fire restrictions. A loophole exists in that if a trekker sleeps in a Sherpa lodge, cooking with firewood is permitted. Hot showers and washing clothes follows. The difficulty with non compliance applies to many, from residents desiring a ready source of cash to employees and visitors, including government liaison officers, who want the warmth and comfort of an open fire to soften the relative harshness of the environment.

Coburn goes on to suggest that waves of refugees from Tibet have added to the population pressure caused by tourists and expeditions. He points out that increased wealth has been followed by increased grazing — the yak and its hybrid cousins are seen as symbols of prosperity and a natural channel of investment for the upwardly mobile. Unfortunately, the extra animals ate the grass to the ground causing the eventual dissemination of the herds. Even with the collaboration of the World Heritage Foundation and the New Zealand Government, the pastures and forests are still teetering on the brink of survival. If forest cover is thinned by as much as 40−50 per cent, soil and water protective ability is lost as water can pass through a thinned-out forest with the same ease as if all the trees had been removed. This is particularly so with over-grazing.

If the rest of the country, unrestrained by the strict and some-times openly resented rules of the Sagarmatha National Park, continues to consume wood at the present rate, all the commercial forests — 12 per cent of the total — will be gone in ten years, according to H.C. Reiger. Geologically, young soil of the Himalayas is all too easily eroded — giving rise to the grim joke 'the country's leading export is soil'. Unforested hills, unprotected from torrential rain, can rapidly become unproductive. As it takes 600 years to produce 2.5 cm (1 in) of topsoil, it is not hard to imagine Nepal becoming a new Afghanistan in 50 years time.

With these facts in mind we became even more convinced that small is beautiful and the two-to-four person expedition was a necessary step that we as climbers could personally make to help preserve the environment that we loved so much.

Exhausted from the excitement of preparations for the trip and suffering from jetlag, we flopped down on the bumpy, hard mattresses and greyish sheets of our bona fide, one-star hotel, the Himalayan View. A carefully framed certificate hung proudly in the foyer testifying that the hotel had attained this awesome stature. Chosen not for its view but for its cheap prices and central location, we also reaped the benefits of the management's experienced dealings with rather eccentric climbers and the inordinate amount of paraphernalia that inevitably follow them. For providing endless cups of tea, sweetened with patience and understanding, for the half dozen expeditions that passed through its doors during our stay, we awarded them a five-star rating.

Night came on the 14th day of the waning moon; it was Shiv Ratri, or the sacred night's celebration of Lord Shiva. As many as 100,000 worshippers would pass though the gates of Pashupatinath, the most sacred of Hindu shrines, on the shores of the Bhagmati River. Caught up in the explosive atmosphere generated by the pilgrims arriving by bus, plane and on foot, we jumped onto our hired bicycles and sped through the night to get amongst it all, tiredness melting away in the crisp air.

On the way I entertained Chris with raunchy stories of how phallic worship was explained in religious texts, described by Anderson in *Festivals of Nepal*. Shiva was making love to his wife — but was disturbed by Brahma, Vishnu and other gods. Far from being disconcerted, his inhibitions dulled from excessive alcohol, Shiva continued to gratify his desires. When sobriety finally came, the visitors disclosed the sordid truth. The words 'fell like a clap of thunder' and both Shiva and his wife died in the position the visitors found them. Shiva, being immortal, made the proclamation that the very act that brought about his shame and death should now be celebrated, claiming that to honour him through the symbol of the lingam would undoubtedly secure a place in heaven for the pious.

I went on to describe another legend of how Vishnu and Brahma were quarrelling over who was supreme. A glorious fiery lingam arose without beginning, middle or end. 'That's hard to beat,' Chris commented wryly. I ignored his remark and continued with Anderson's description: 'Vishnu, determined to find the source of this blinding column, became a giant boar and plunged downwards, but after travelling for 1,000 years still no base could be found. Brahma became a swan and, swift as thought, travelled upwards seeking the pillar's end, but was equally unsuccessful. When Shiva appeared before the two exhausted gods they bowed before him to make the sacred sound of "om". Shiva thereby established his supremacy and the symbol of his lingam in the three worlds.'

By now we had arrived in the groves of trees that surrounded the temple. Sardus, or Indian holy men, dressed only in ragged loincloths, their bodies smeared with ashes (often those of cremated people), crouched around open fires. Flames lit up their faces, gaunt from fasting and the long journey. Some had prostrated themselves the entire distance from the Gangetic Plain, through the Maharbharat Range to the Kathmandu Valley, their journey taking probably a year or more to complete. In order to protect their hands and knees against constant abrasion from rocks and stones, specially constructed wooden pads were worn. Their drive and singularity of purpose towards enlightenment was awesome. Matted long hair stuck out wildly, framing the cutting intensity of their staring black eyes. We returned to an ugly square cement box that was our hotel room.

The next morning we assembled to meet our hired staff through Sherpa Co-operative Trekking P. Ltd. Our sardar, or head Sherpa, was called Kusang. A heavy-set man of Tibetan descent with thick features, he had some experience carrying loads at high altitude. As we only required someone to assist us carrying loads through the long moraine and lower part of the mountain, we were not too concerned about his climbing abilities, as long as he was able to climb out of a crevasse, should he fall in one. He appeared perfectly adequate for our needs. Sangay was our cook. A Sherpa in his mid-twenties, he was very finely built, his features more artistic than Kusang's. He looked unlikely as a budding mountain climber but he certainly seemed to have the potential to be an excellent cook, as he assured us he was.

At the last moment a young boy who had been lingering in the background was pushed forward by his friends, his courage seeming to have failed. The shy applicant was after the job of kitchen boy and mail runner. We were taken aback a little, not realising the position was being offered. Chris squirmed uncomfortably at the thought of adding yet another body, another mouth to feed and another unknown factor to our rapidly growing contingent. When Mike Cheney — the agent who worked on our behalf through Sherpa Co-op — reiterated that the job of food preparation is quite involved, starting from having to walk some distance to collect water from a stream to the lengthy process of cooking rice, lentils, vegetables and meat over an open fire, and finishing with the cleaning of the pots and pans, we saw the reasoning and conceded to the popular consensus. In addition, it was pointed out that even though we expected no mail ourselves, we were required to submit weekly reports of our progress to His Majesty's Government. Cheney's addition would facilitate communication and also allow fresh food and supplies to be brought up from the nearest town of Ghunsa on his return run. It turned out to be one of the best decisions we made on the entire trip.

Sanglai was also in his mid-twenties with a quick and ready smile and sparkling brown eyes. He radiated warmth and spontaneity. At about 1.62 m (5 ft 4 in) tall, with the same broad foot and high instep as mine, our shoe sizes and body build matched almost identically. We had no trouble fitting him out with suitable foot-ware and clothing — he just wore my extra stuff. Sanglai was a Tamang — his origins were thought to be Tibetan, similar to the Sherpas. Consequently, he had the same Mongoloid-type features although he lacked the epicanthic fold. The Tamang, Sherpa and Tibetan languages are equally unintelligible to each other and the four races represented in our small group conversed in the national language, Nepali, which they had learnt in school. However, Mike counselled us not to practise our Nepali with them but to use English to encourage them to develop their skill with the language. It was an indispensible tool for their advancement in the tourist industry. We of course agreed, having plenty of opportunity to claim other victims with whom we could speak Nepali.

A police officer was assigned to act as our liaison officer. A mild mannered man of Hindu religion named Bishnu Shrestha, his countenance was so shy and gentle we wondered how effective he would be in the role of translator and mediator with the local people, should we have difficulties either with theft or porter strikes. Nonetheless he was an amiable character, and as a representative of His Majesty's Government it was his role to make sure we obeyed the rules set down for mountaineering teams. These were too numerous to remember and we constantly found ourselves consulting the handbook provided. They ranged from providing adequate clothing, shelter and set wages to ensuring we did not stray from our predetermined objective and cross over into Tibet, temptingly close at hand and easily accessible. This was probably not an unreasonable rule considering Nepal's delicate relations with China and its desire to promote tourism, at the same time as wishing to avoid an international incident at all costs. The penalties were high: being banned from climbing in Nepal for a minimum of five years, possibly affecting not only oneself but also the country one represented; it would make the violator an unpopular figure back home.

Pasang Kami, an old friend of both Chris and myself, met us at Sherpa Co-op as we were about to distribute the necessary equipment for our staff. A Sherpa from the Khumbu region and a veteran climber, Pasang was a remarkably sophisticated person, often in striking contrast to his peers. Ten years ago he had stayed at my home on Chobar to recuperate from a typically western malady, a peptic ulcer. Sensitive and highly strung, his exceptional intelligence and organisational abilities meant that he was one of the most sought-after Sherpas. The cost was telling. His gaunt features and hyperactivity showed that perhaps he was on the first seat of a roller coaster with barely a second to glance over his shoulder to see from whence he had come. Sadness looked quietly through the windows of his eyes as he wished us well. Certain of the knowledge that so many of his friends had met their destiny in the icy wastes of the Himalayas, 'Don't take any unnecessary risks!', he cautioned, 'it's just not worth it.' 'Don't worry Pasang, we'll come back.' Somehow, all three of us knew that inevitably we would take risks and were not at all sure if we would return.

We turned to look at the gear spread out in neat piles covering the floor of the room. Long underwear, woollen pants, shirts, sweaters, down jackets, single and double boots, ice axes and crampons, sleeping bags and rucksacks. Brand new and the best quality generously provided by equipment suppliers in the States, it represented an enormous amount of work and expense. We held our breath as Kusang and Sangay fingered through the piles, like children emptying the contents of a Christmas stocking, with us the parents looking on. Rather than checking the sizes to see if the clothing fitted, we noticed them checking brand names, 'Is this Gortex?' Rather apologetically Chris answered, 'Er, no it's not, we've found ...' He was cut short, 'Japanese expedition, everyone have Gortex sleeping bag.' Our hearts sank. 'Well, Kusang, we're not the Japanese. You have the same quality bag as ours and we are more than happy with them.' It was a widely spread practice for Sherpas to take the newly issued equipment and sell it in the local market, taking along instead their old equipment that may have seen many an expedition. Pasang, Chris and I exchanged glances, fully aware of the materialism and greed that had crept into a once naive and innocent people.

At one time this hard working, industrious and hardy people were exploited by expeditions, they were often led into a harsh environment without proper clothing or shelter. Many perished or were severely frostbitten. As a result, rules and regulations were set by the Department of Tourism to prevent such abuses, such as mandatory life insurance policies for the families of the survivors, provided by the climbers. Now it seemed the pendulum was swinging in the opposite direction. As a small and mostly privately funded trip, we were hard-pressed to compete against a large expedition, such as the Japanese, backed by newspaper corporations with fancy gear and gimmicks. Amongst other things we had overlooked as important 'baksheesh' (or bonus) items were Levi jeans and Nike running shoes, brand specific. We agreed to pay extra rupees to reach a harmonious agreement and they took off to the bazaar to buy last-minute kitchen utensils and other miscellaneous items. With a final briefing at the ministry with the liaison officer Bishnu, our bus tickets were purchased for early the following morning. Our business in Kathmandu had reached an end.

The only weakness in the armour of hanging ice cliffs was a 120 m (400 ft) ice gully that led to the first snow terrace. Ninety metres (300 ft) of fixed line was used on this section.

4

*Life leads the thoughtful man on a path of many
windings. Now the course is checked, now it runs
straight again. Here winged thoughts may pour freely
forth in words. There the heavy burden of knowledge
must be shut away in silence.*

*But when two people are at one in their inmost
hearts, they shatter even the strength of bronze and
iron, and when two people understand each other in
their inmost hearts, their words are strong and sweet
like the fragrance of orchids.*

I CHING

IT WAS STILL dark when we gathered at the bus station. Eighteen
loads for our expedition had been carefully stacked on top of the
bus and tied down. We were to purchase the rest of our food in
Dharan, 352 km (220 miles) away in far eastern Nepal. Ahead lay an
18-hour journey, providing there were no mechanical breakdowns.
We would be sharing this pleasure — and the approach march to the
mountain — with another expedition, an eight-member Spanish
team on their way to Jannu, another part of the Kanchenjunga
massif. Unable to communicate more than a few words, we just
exchanged smiles and handshakes.

In addition to the Spanish, our bus companions included a rich
assortment of local people laden down with their personal belongings. One couple were obviously newlywed, decked out in their
finest clothing and jewellery, she in a blood-red sari trimmed with
gold. The girl was painfully shy and kept her dark eyes lowered,
avoiding eye contact with anyone. This is regarded as right and

*Taking advantage of a shallow crevasse saved the considerable labour of digging a
snow cave at 7,000 m (23,000 ft). With one side missing, we are treated to an
expansive panorama of the Tibetan plateau. (Photo Chris Chandler)*

proper behaviour; a girl who talks too much or laughs a lot in the company of men is open to question about her fidelity. In spite of the studied avoidance of contact with each other I sensed the excitement and tension the couple shared wordlessly. Perhaps this was a union of love rather than parents' choice, where compatability takes second place to caste and social standing. For the young girl, there was also the ominous thought of leaving her family's house where she was loved and respected, to enter her husband's house where her role would change dramatically. Under the often harsh supervision of her mother-in-law and possible co-wives, she would be on the lowest level of the household, in function little better than a servant. Only the birth of a son would elevate her from this lowly position. A cow, a bed and a chest of clothes and jewellery were the essentials of a dowry, depending on the wealth of the girl's parents. I had never heard of a case of a wife being doused in petrol then set alight, as sometimes happens in India when the in-laws consider the dowry to be insufficient. Nonetheless her future was uncertain and fraught with difficulties. I wished her well. A small goat accompanied them on board. I was pleased it was not a cow!

We were lucky to have reserved seats as many stood in the aisle or rode on the roof. Finally the bus, sagging under the weight it carried, lurched forward and we took off along the winding road which led south through the Maharbharat Range and Siwalik foothills to the flat lands of the Terai. Politically part of Nepal but geographically an extension of the Gangetic Plain, the Terai was once uninhabitable due to a particularly virulent form of malaria carried by mosquitoes that bred in the lush jungles. Following the heavy use of DDT the disease has essentially been eliminated. Because of the shrinking amount of arable land in the foothills following forest denudation and massive soil erosion, there has been a large scale migration of hills people to the relatively fertile flatlands of the Terai. Slash-and-burn agriculture and government projects of commercial logging had removed the sal forests of the jungle. Tiger, elephant and one-horned rhinoceros were among the casualties but now they are protected. In the eastern Terai, 83,000 hectares (205,000 acres) of forest remain of 258,200 hectares (638,300 acres) that existed in 1928, according to Harker Gurung.

The tragedy deepens when one learns that it is the more enterprising who depart the villages of the foothills, leaving behind the aged and dispirited who are unable to prevent the spiral of decline. These changes occurred in only a few decades.

Our bodies gradually adjusted to the violence of the bus careering through potholes and ruts in the road, as though they were non-existent. Occasionally, a head caught off-guard rammed full-force into the overhead rack. 'You snooze, you lose' became the motto for survival.

Several hours passed and we pulled up to what would be the Californian equivalent of a fast-food restaurant on the off-ramp of a freeway. A shelter of sunbaked mud-brick walls with a thatched straw roof, furnished with a number of rough-hewn tables and chairs, were clues to the fact that it was an eating house. In the corner, several large aluminium pots sat over an open hearth and various kinds of fried breads and sweets sat in the open sun. Flies hovered in the dust-filled air. Open drains carrying raw sewage lay feet away from food preparation. My stomach gave a somersault. We were not over culture shock yet. Chris had surveyed the scene and done some shopping of his own; he placed two eggs on the table. 'Take a look at these, I thought they might be cleaner to eat, but the shells are quite soft. I've never seen anything like it.' 'I think the chickens were fed DDT-contaminated grain, I wouldn't touch them,' I replied. He gave me a horrified look and pushed them aside. 'Just make sure our plates are clean and dry, and if we only eat food straight out of the pot over the fire, maybe we can be lucky enough to avoid getting sick,' I cautioned. After the meal we went outside to see the vendor with the suspect merchandise. His price was half that of normal eggs but in spite of this the local people were not buying them. I was relieved.

Back in the bus again the return of the now familiar bumps and jolts reminded me that I had been avoiding an important reality of life: my bladder was incapable of holding another ounce of fluid. For men it was a relatively simple matter, but I had better observe the womenfolk among my fellow passengers to see how they coped. For the first-time visitor to Nepal, the indiscriminate defecation of its inhabitants is one of the most striking impressions one receives, along with the total disregard for sanitation at all levels of

Nepalese society. The failure to recognise the link between a fly laying larva on a nearby stool then landing directly on a plate of food, makes even the most sheltered short-term visitor unlikely to escape annoying and sometimes debilitating gastro-intestinal problems. Those most commonly responsible for illness and decreased productivity are amoeba, roundworm, giardiasis and other parasites such as hookworm and pinworm.

Well-intentioned foreign aid projects designed to improve sanitation have failed for a variety of reasons, both cultural and practical. B.A. Coburn states that inadequate water supply, insufficient means to meet the demands, irregular or no maintenance are all obstacles. The odious job of hand cleaning the repositories that do exist is left to the lowest caste, the 'untouchables', who at times must literally immerse themselves in their medium. Widespread distaste for defecating in the same place makes change difficult to implement, as latrines are thought of as areas of collected filth. The fear that dogs will go undernourished and an important need to examine their stool for parasites are other causes that Coburn gives for failure to implement change. A widespread and crippling embarrassment over the subject compounds the entire problem. Before the installation of Biogas latrines in Patan, a relatively small compound served as a community defecation area for thousands of women a day. Fetid pools of accumulated waste lay 30 cm (1 ft) deep, with small stepping stones for convenience. The liquid waste flowed into a small stream, the same stream where the women cleaned themselves. By comparison, the men's area was far less crowded and fresher water was available. I wept at the thought of it. Blissfully unaware, the tiny goat beside me felt the urge and released its load on my foot. I felt envious.

The miles rolled on. We stopped again. I followed several women as discreetly as possible and did what I had to without the protective modesty of a sari. Gagging several times, I wandered back to the waiting bus in a daze. My eyes caught an exquisitely beautiful girl in a pink sari bending down for some water. The transparent fabric of her sari clung to her body as she stood up, revealing a figure designed for the centrefold of *Playboy* magazine. Captivated, I stared without reservation. 'Truly a lotus blooming on the dung pile,' I mused. I turned to search for a place to sit. In doing so I noticed the entire Spanish expedition and both liaison officers transfixed, mouths open, looking in her direction. Chris had joined the reverie along with every male passenger in the bus. The women were more guarded, casting only fleeting glances. Nobody escaped her power.

Suddenly my stomach gave a triple somersault. Maybe I was coming down with something? We all trooped back into the bus. Eight hours to go. Bonded by our mutual discomforts and common goal of Dharan, the busload was now united by the memory of the nymph-like figure by a water fountain. The bus became a hydroplane and we took off on a cushion of air as the spell of her beauty lingered. Suspended in the delightful state between dream and sleep I soon took on her magical qualities and sought out Chris to seduce him in my dreams. Before I knew it, we had arrived at Dharan. Chris leant over and whispered in my ear, 'I dreamt of you the whole way.' I thanked him secretly.

The task of buying the remainder of our fresh and dried food supplies completed, we were assured by Kusang and Sangay that we had sufficient supplies to cover the 18-day trek to the mountain and also six weeks' sojourn at Base Camp. It was understood that we would supplement the basic rations with chicken and fresh vegetables as they became available along the trail. Sufficient kerosene was purchased to cover our entire cooking needs for the trip. We would either wash in cold water or, more ideally, let the grease build up to a comfortable level, providing protection and insulation against the cold. In practice, vanity inevitably got the better of me and I'd succumb to washing my hair, sometimes at sub-zero temperatures. This created the annoying problem of not being able to brush it because it had frozen solid.

Following on the heels of a larger expedition had several drawbacks as we proceeded to hire our porters. Afraid we wouldn't be able to attract sufficient number, Kusang persuaded us to make the loads an attactive 5−7 kg (10−15 lb) lighter than the government-regulated standard of 33 kg (66 lb). Chris and I were impatient to get going and wished to take as little time as possible to reach Base Camp. We proposed to stage 'double-day' carries, (walking twice the normal distance), as much as possible, but pay the porters as though they had taken 18 days, plus an additional bonus for incentive. This plan was rejected by Kusang — apparently everyone except us preferred to walk in a single group. There was little we could do but accept the majority rule. Finally it was agreed to make the carry in 17 days.

Two industrious fellows wished to carry double loads for double the money. At 24 rupees a day for carrying 28 kg (56 lb), this amounted to about $1.50 per day, a bargain for us. Nonetheless it was probably more than twice the amount the same fellows could expect to earn portering for local people. A field worker was paid as little as six rupees a day, plus food, for planting and harvesting. A woman could expect half that. We were acutely aware of the problem of luring much-needed hands from the fields to the more lucrative job of portering for foreigners, thereby leaving the fields unattended. With a large expedition or even one of modest size, this presents a serious problem.

We all set out together — 60–70 porters from the Spanish expedition and our contingent of 21. The Spanish group's liaison officer had discovered my age was several years more than Chris's and took great delight in pointing out this fact. It was an undoubted stigma, judging by the gleam in his eye. He had come from the same village of Chainpur that Terry, my first husband, had served in as a peace corp volunteer. The knowledge of our divorce probably added more vehemence to his comments. 'What a jerk!', I commented to Chris. 'There just doesn't seem to be any getting away from it!' To divorce an incompatible mate was almost unheard of in Hindu society; the couple would remain outcasts of their village.

Lynn Bennet, in her book *Dangerous Wives and Sacred Sisters*, explains that the path of the Hindu ascetic to divine enlightenment is one of denial of the body's desires and needs, which are seen as stumbling blocks along the way. The village householder, as the opposite to the ascetic, is immersed in the process of contributing to ongoing life. Though their paths are different, their goals are the same. The villager's concern lies in observing strict controls over the processes of eating, copulation, elimination, menstruation, birth and death, and attempting to purify their polluting effects. In this way, through the process of many rebirths, he can hope to reach Nirvana. The submersion of women to a position of powerlessness and lowliness is the Hindu's way of keeping a woman's sexuality in tight control. Hindu thought is heavy with the belief that sexuality undermines and destroys spiritual power gained through ascetic practices.

Lynn Bennet goes on to reveal that it is the women who preserve the pedigree of the offspring by foregoing relations outside caste and marriage boundaries. On a deeper level the woman becomes the controller of the spiritual purity of the children by her fidelity. Though treated by all as powerless, therein lies all the power, largely unrecognised by even the women themselves. Instead, Hindu women are inheritors of a legacy that focuses on their potential defilement. This is brought to full attention by the annual ritual Rishi Pancami, described and participated in by Bennet. This ritual bathing is designed to purify a woman from the possible sin of having touched a man whilst menstruating. At early dawn by the riverside, the woman rubs her genitals 360 times with red mud. Feet, knees, elbows, armpits and forehead follow. The entire process is followed by white mud and then cow dung. The whole event culminates in the woman paying her husband the most extreme form of respect, that of washing his feet then drinking the water. This act and that of eating only food left over from the unwashed plate of the husband are symbolic statements. The husband is so high above the wife that even his impurities are pure for her.

Clearly, western women present an enigma to Hindu men. The hostility of the Spanish group's liaison officer was softened by our own liaison officer, Bishnu, with whom I shared an amicable relationship. I was cast in the role of a sister, revered and respected, yet clearly off limits. It was comfortable for both of us.

The trail out of Dharan wound up a parched hill to the town of Dhankuta, situated on the crest of a ridge at about 1,800 m (6,000 ft). Along the way we passed a continual stream of people carrying all manner of goods and merchandise. So thick was the foot traffic that there were often traffic jams. A long trail of porters carried a length of cable probably 150 m (500 ft) long and 8 cm (3 in) thick, for use in the construction of a suspension bridge to span the Tamur River. Without roads, how could one transport such enormous weight and bulk? By ingenuity and dogged determination! Uncoiled, with a porter supporting the cable every 3–6 m (10–20 ft), it was carried patiently on their shoulders. To facilitate rest stops, a supervisor was posted every 15 m (50 ft) or so with a whistle. When the decision to stop was made by the head man, the whistle signal was given and repeated in quick succession by the supervisors placed along the entire length, creating a ripple-like effect as the men lowered their burden to rest on a V-shaped stick, carried specially for the purpose.

It was part of an ambitious British Foreign Aid Project to construct a road which would link Dharan to Hille and eventually span the entire 322 km (200 mile) stretch across the eastern midlands of Nepal to link with Dhologhat, just outside Kathmandu. Leading a developing country into the 21st century is fraught with difficulties and almost everyone can see the benefits of road construction in a country which up to a few years ago, had none. Improved communication, transport of goods and troops in the event of invasion are among the more obvious gains, and keenly desired by the king as a necessary step to the future.

We stopped to share a few beers with the road engineers, British advisers to the project. Their ideas, probably intensified by long periods of isolation from their own culture and burnt out by the effects of the snail-like pace of progress, were strikingly different from what we expected. As self-described mercenaries, for no other reason than that they were being well paid, they felt that constructing a road through this fragile environment was raping the land. I recognised that beneath the facade of cynicism lay a desire to do the very best job possible and the feeling that if they withdrew, someone less competent might take over and really mess up.

One of the engineers pointed out that the road lay in one of the most seismically active areas in Asia and crossed over and followed a major fault line. We began to understand the problems of landslides and erosion that would constantly plague the road. He went on to explain that the reason progress had been so painstakingly slow was that they were constantly delayed by having to maintain the small section of road that had already been built. His companion then described a road built in 1947, 15 km (9 miles) long, from Gantok to Nathu La on the Tibet border. It was through one of the densest rhododendron forests in the world with 500 cm (200 in) of rainfall a year. Ten years after the road was built not one tree stood there. Obviously soil conservation needed to go hand in hand with road construction unless a heavy economic and ecological price was to be paid.

Many men, women and even small children squatted beside the road with a large pile of rocks in front of them. It was their job to turn the large rocks into fine gravel by the unbelievably tedious task of breaking the stones with a small sledge-hammer. The men broke the larger rocks which they passed to the women who made them smaller. Children and the aged finished them off, and the final piles were of remarkably uniform size. Another train of workers with straw baskets carried the gravel to a predesignated point. The sides of the road where it cut through the hillsides were all carefully reinforced with a mosaic of stones of intermediate size, then covered with wire mesh.

Large, well-constructed drains were sited at frequent intervals in anticipation of the monsoon downpours. There appeared to be meticulous attention to detail, but then I am not a civil engineer. I did notice the hills were largely bare of trees and sparsely covered with grass. The whole place had the well ordered and industrious atmosphere of an ant colony that had just discovered the carcass of a dead elephant.

I sank into a dispirited melancholy. What could we as individuals do about such problems? Was there even a solution? Sitting under the large pipal tree that marked a resting spot for porters above the town of Dhankuta, Chris and I cooled ourselves in the welcome breeze and mulled over the considerations and priorities that a leader of a country such as Nepal must decide upon. 'There is only one Himalaya to lose' — the words of Hans Reiger rang in the crisp air.

The next day's walk brought us to the delightful town of Hille, a hamlet of prosperous Tibetan-speaking traders and storekeepers. The place had a look of scrubbed cleanliness. The streets were paved with stone, the houses had freshly whitewashed walls and bright red, mud verandahs. On patios, babies rocked in cradles, women sunned themselves, children played, dogs barked. Curious eyes peeked from elaborately carved windows. We sucked on fresh mandarins and relaxed.

I was pleased to discover a woodcarver in the house next door to where we were staying. He had just come from Tibet via Walung-chung Gola, and displayed exceptional skill. I had done some woodcarving under the tutorage of a Sherpa friend whilst living in Kathmandu, and still had a keen interest. It was inspiring to watch him work and good to know that the arts were still alive and sought after, and talent recognised. He had made the long journey to Hille to work on a special commission for a wealthy merchant.

Hille sits at about 2,100 m (7,000 ft) on a ridge crest which winds its way in a north easterly direction to a maximum height of 3,000 m (10,000 ft), eventually to drop dramatically 1,800 m (6,000 ft) into the Tamur River valley at Dobhan. It marks the stepping-off point for one of the most beautiful walks in the world.

The days were artificially short and sometimes we walked for only three hours before Kusang called a halt. The reason he gave was lack of water, which to a certain extent was true. There were remarkably few springs, which probably accounted for the scantily populated settlements that clustered around the available water, which was sometimes fouled by cattle.

Despite the lack of ground water, the forests of rhododendron, oak, hemlock, laurel and maple stood tall and dense enough to create their own atmosphere of humidity, and support luxuriant ferns and thick masses of orchids from almost every branch. A rolling sea of rhododendron blossoms ranging in colour from deep red to white lay like foam on the green waves of trees, interspersed with thickets of magnolia — a sure sign of spring. A sudden flurry of movement in the underbrush signalled a fleeting glimpse of the trailing feathers of pheasants in flight. The steepest ravines were the most densely forested and promised the greatest treasures: echoing bird calls and the chattering of monkeys to lure us to the ravine edges. Chris entertained me by starting up a dialogue with a bird, answering its call in almost perfect imitation. Certainly well enough to fool the puzzled bird.

To the west lay the Arun River valley giving spectacular views of Makalu, 8,481 m (27,824 ft); Chamlang, 7,319 m (24,012 ft); Baruntse, 7,220 m (23,687 ft); Everest, 8,848 m (29,028 ft); Lhotse, 8,511 m (27,922 ft); and Lhotse Shar, 8,383 m (27,502 ft) some 110 km (70 miles) away. To the north east lay the Tamur River leading to the Kanchenjunga massif, a mere 80 km (50 miles) away as the crow flies. Sunrise and sunset were very special times to seek out a sheltered glade on a rock to absorb the beauty that surrounded us.

The Nepalis are generally afraid of the forests and do not like to stray too far from the village or the paths. Forest spirits, bandits and wild animals are the reasons for this fear. We met a man on the trail whose nose had been bitten off by the most feared of all animals — the Himalayan black bear. Years earlier, on the approach to Dhaulagiri, I came across another poor man whose jaw had been ripped off with a single swipe of the bear's powerful paws. Because of the resulting disfigurement he wore a cloth draped across his face. Fearless and aggressive, the black bear has a reputation for raiding crops and livestock. In recent years I do not think this has been much of a problem, but the fear remains.

Hans Reiger, in *Man vs Mountain*, gives an explanation other than fear for the seemingly mindless lopping of trees which eventually denudes them of all their branches and gives them such a peculiar shape. He calls it 'the green apple picking syndrome'. 'Consider an apple which is not ripe. If the tree is privately owned then the owner will wait until the fruit is ripe before picking, but if the tree is commonly owned, the apples will be most likely picked green and all the earlier, the greater the competition. This explains why, if a tree is spared by an individual, another may come and cut its leaves for fodder. This very expectation makes it rational for the first man to make the first step.

'The second variant is the collective action dilemma, best explained by the spectator-seating problem. In a crowded stadium spectators generally stand, although if they sat down everybody would be better off. The first individual to sit down would not see anything at all, so it is rational for him to remain standing.' Reiger gives this as an example of the overgrazing of forest areas desperately in need of regeneration. Nobody makes the first move to restrict cattle from grazing in the area because in doing so, he would lose a grazing opportunity whilst his neighbours profit from reduced grazing density.

The signs of man's encroachment on even this relatively sparsely populated forest were telling — not only by the cutting of branches but also by the well worn trails along which we were walking; they were deeply eroded, by as much as 2 m (6 ft) into the hillside.

Reiger points out that it would be a mistake to think that Nepalis do not realise the effects of their actions on the forests and farmlands. The tragedy is that they are forced to continue with a certain pattern of behaviour because there appears to be no viable alternative.

As we descended the ridge into the Tamur Valley the forest was left behind and we passed through terraced paddy fields. The main crop is rice, transplanted on the irrigated lower fields before the onset of the monsoon and harvested four months later. Corn is planted in early spring. Barley, millet and soy beans are other crops. Winter wheat is planted in the autumn, potatoes in January. Chris and I wandered through the maze of paths that lead through the paddies and often found ourselves separated from the main caravan — usually by choice. Kusang had a habit of making us feel 'in the way'. He obviously enjoyed the power and authority of his position which Chris's presence seemed to undermine. We would do spot checks on our loads several times a day but it was impossible and probably unnecessary to watch everyone at all times. There was some uneasiness, however, especially since the Spanish had their loads locked and sealed in pilfer-proof containers, whilst ours were unlocked, contained in straw baskets or duffle bags. We were relying heavily on the 'honour system' and hoped it would work.

Accustomed to going on ahead of the porters, we found we had taken the wrong trail altogether. It came as a surprise to look down about 300 m (1,000 ft) and see our porters and familiar blue duffles winding their way on a trail along the valley floor out of Dobhan. Chris was interrupted by a sudden call of nature. He took off to search for a secluded spot. I sat down on a rock to wait, welcoming the rest. It seemed he had been gone for ever and I began to feel a growing concern — perhaps he was having severe stomach cramps? I got up and walked in the direction he had disappeared. Suddenly I saw his blond head pop up with a very unhappy expression. 'What's wrong — you took so long ... do you feel sick?' 'You wouldn't believe what happened, Cherie. I saw this ideal place, it wasn't on a field and well off the trail, surrounded with bushes for privacy. The urgency of the situation was becoming overpowering so I quickly went about my business. No sooner had I finished when this Sadhu fellow — naked except for a loincloth — appears out of nowhere and starts yelling at me. He's really upset. It seems I shit in his little worshipping spot! Oh, he was so mad he was fit to be tied. I did my best to apologise and clean up the mess. But what could I really do, I just felt awful.'

Chris needed consoling, but quite inappropriately I began to giggle and then laugh. I couldn't help it, the tears rolled down my cheeks as I imagined the whole scenario. Here we were, the two of us trying to be so 'culturally sensitive' and he had just committed about the worst possible act. Chris did not exactly join in my hilarity but it did make him feel a little lighter. 'Just think about it, Chris, you gave him a once-in-a-lifetime opportunity to meditate on your shit. Maybe this was his chance to reach enlightenment, "to fashion stars out of dog dung". Now that is Great Work.'

We moved on towards the mountain of our dreams. Over the next six days our caravan climbed gradually from an altitude of 1,200 m (4,000 ft) to distinctly Buddhist country, characterised by fluttering, tall, prayer flags. Strips of cotton printed with wood-block impressions carried blessings to all living creatures. At 3,500 m (11,500 ft) the village of Pele sat nestled among small plots of land bounded by squat stone walls. A monastery on the hillside was a necessary stopping point for Sanglai who was most concerned that we offer gifts and receive the lama's blessings. As a talisman for one, or an abstract symbol for another, we all received a length of red cotton thread that was tied around our necks to ensure safety for our coming venture. We paid our respects to the wisdom the lama embodied and departed for Ghunsa, a mere 150 m (500 ft) higher. We left amidst the fading sounds of the monks' chanting, immersed in the strange feeling evoked by the cacophony of ringing bells, clashing cymbals and blowing of conch shells.

Ghunsa marked the turning point for our scantily clad, low altitude porters who, shivering miserably, looked clearly out of place among these stocky, high-cheekboned, jovial people, clad in traditional sack-like robes of heavy yak wool, brightly coloured aprons and necklaces of amber and turquoise.

Pay-off time took on the solemnity of religious ritual. Signing acknowledgement of money received was accomplished by a thumb print, blackened on the charred bottom of a frying pan. Each porter took meticulous care not to smudge the impression, otherwise it had to be repeated. The crisp notes were carefully inspected and counted. Discovering a small bonus sent them whooping out of the door in wild leaps. Their yells of joy could be heard all the way down the valley.

The Spanish took off for Jannu Base Camp while we elected for a day of rest and acclimatisation. This pause allowed us to take stock of our situation. Kusang's and, to some extent, Sangay's sullen behaviour was becoming of increasing concern. Not only was Kusang's honesty in question but his overbearing manner was hard to deal with. Chris had kept careful records of all money handed to Kusang for lodgings, cooking and food expenses along the way, but when asked to account for the money spent, he consistently came up hundreds of rupees short. We dismissed it as a mind sloppy to the details of bookkeeping, but the underlying antagonistic attitude to questioning was worrying. That afternoon, Kusang really overstepped the limit.

As the nearest medical care was in Tapeljung, seven days' walk away, we were inundated with people seeking medical care and advice. In the midst of women holding sick infants in their arms, he jumped up on the verandah and announced that this was 'bad medicine' and ordered them to stay away from us and told us to go to our tent! Aware of a recent scandal in India where a certain drug company had knowingly dispensed long outdated tetracycline, causing severe side effects and even death, we tried to be reassuring. Clearly, everyone was confused and embarrassed by the scene. We chose to ignore Kusang, while Bishnu continued patiently translating the various symptoms of bronchitis, conjunctivitis, ear infections, abscessed teeth and gastro-intestinal disease. We felt satisfied that at least some people had been helped, but at the same time humbled by the knowledge that we provided at best a 'quickie-cure', as nothing had been done to touch on the underlying causes of disease: poor sanitation and hygiene. We tried to lace the medicine with as much health care teaching as possible, stressing the simple act of hand washing.

Retiring to the privacy of our tent to mellow out, we talked over the problem of how best to handle Kusang. A 'watch and wait' policy was adopted. As it was important that we have people we could rely on during our long absences on the mountain, I won-

APPROACH MARCH TO KANCHENJUNGA

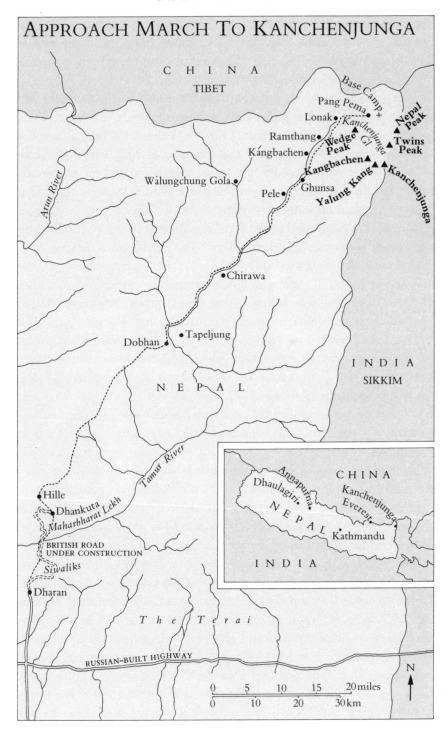

dered how it would work out. Our attention was drawn to the now familiar, monotonous tones of a mantra recitation and the occasional sounds of a ringing bell, the symbol of impermanence. Just as the sounds of a bell are fleeting and cannot be retained, so too is human life. I stuck my head out of the door to discover an old woman in her seventies circumambulating our tent, a prayer wheel in one hand, a bell in the other. Old age in that culture is a time for introspection, to see through the illusions of life. It is a time of pride in one's achievements. Given an elevated status in society the aged are allowed to retire from customary duties, often becoming monks or nuns in order to prepare for the coming transition of death. This woman had taken a strong interest in the two of us and was most concerned for our safety. The circumambulations continued over the next two days whenever we were in the tent. She stopped at nightfall. We tried not to attach too great a significance to her actions, we were even a little embarrassed, but concentrated on the kindness of her heart represented by her actions.

Our loads were now transferred to that most charismatic of all creatures, the yak. To be more precise, these animals were dzo, yaks crossbred with cattle to make them easier to handle and capable of producing more milk. The yak can be a rather wild and troublesome beast of burden and his cousin only a little less so, judging by the problems the head yak man and his son had in loading up the animals.

Excitement was scarcely containable as we wound our way through lush alpine meadows sprinkled with delicate gentians, poppies and primulas, braving the remnants of snow that still lay in shaded glades. It was difficult to imagine how the icy blasts of wind did not cause their beauty to wither and die.

The snout of the Kanchenjunga glacier was now at our feet as the trail over grass-covered moraine led by the awesome north face of Jannu. Several days travel brought us past Kangbachen and Ramthang to Lonak, which marked the junction of another broad valley that led over an easy pass into Tibet. For centuries traders, pilgrims and shepherds had crossed over these high mountain passes with equipment that would make a modern mountaineer pale, namely thick, heavy but almost waterproof and windproof woven yak wool clothing and boots. The soles of the boots were smooth yak hide. They would carry lengths of bamboo as protection against falling into a crevasse, and pulling the hair over eyes prevented snow blindness. Garlic and hashish were thought useful in combating the effects of altitude. Pieces of rock hard cheese were strung into necklaces and sucked to provide stamina and strength. The original map surveys made by Indian pundits Nain Singh and Kishen Singh in 1878 showed just as much ingenuity. Distances measured by counting steps on prayer beads were claimed by their followers to be remarkably accurate.

Three prominent pinnacles of rock pointed out by Sanglai formed a triangle on the wide meadow. They were flanked by an impressive panorama of snow-clad peaks, to contain an especially holy and spiritually rich area, 'Where gods and saints dwell in great numbers', the locals believed. The scene was tranquil.

We climbed a crag and identified the surrounding peaks as Wedge, Nepal, Drohmo I and II, Kangbachen, Yalung Kang and Kanchenjunga. Pulses quickened with excitement as well as with the increased elevation. We were now at 4,900 m (16,000 ft). Tomorrow, 29 March 1981, we would arrive at Base Camp.

5

*As the sun dries the morning dew
So are the sins of man dissipated
At the sight of the Himalaya.*

THE PURANAS

STUNNED BY the beauty and magnitude of the curtains of snow-clad glaciers and cliffs of ice before us, I walked along, tripping over small obstacles in the path, blind to everything but the north face of Kanchenjunga. 'Those wide-angle shots just don't even come close to capturing it, do they Cherie?,' Chris broke the silence. 'We must be insane to tackle something like that, just the two of us,' I whispered. 'Well the best we can do is just go and take a look at it. We're here now,' he concluded.

Pang Pema is situated at about 5,150 m (16,900 ft) at the junction of the Kanchenjunga and Jongsong glaciers, and appeared an ideal location for our Base Camp. It would provide an important refuelling station for the long weeks of gruelling work that lay ahead. Warmth, comfort, running water and grassy meadows provided a place for deer and goat to graze. Their apparent lack of concern about our presence emphasised the remoteness of the area. Curious small rodents scurried among the rocks. Eagles circled overhead, biding time before attack. Pang Pema had it all, including a view that was hard to beat. We had to tear ourselves away from the magic of the mountain to deal with more unpleasant details.

A 'watch-and-wait' policy had been followed in handling the Kusang situation. We were dismayed to find only enough food for two or three weeks, instead of the guaranteed amount of six to eight weeks that we had consistently been told we could rely on. Kusang's jokes on the approach march about leaving Base Camp after two weeks took on a whole new meaning. 'You think his plan was to use up as much food and money in as short a time as possible so that he could just go home?,' I asked Chris pointedly.

'And that accounts for those big rice meals the large family in Ghunsa was eating at the house where we stayed,' I added, remembering that at the time I thought it strange they were not eating their staple food, potatoes. As no rice is grown locally, it tended to be an expensive luxury item. 'Yep, we probably fed the porters the whole trip in. No wonder they were so happy,' Chris commented wryly. 'Either that or the food wasn't even bought in the very beginning.' 'No! — we weighed the loads in the beginning,' remembered Chris. His reactions paralleled mine.

We stayed up all night going over the food and finances record. Kusang's outright deceit and failure to follow our very explicit instructions were obvious. What was equally inexcusable was his increasingly belligerent behaviour — one example was when Chris and I were shut out of the mess tent and had to sit outside for 15 minutes whilst Sangay, Bishnu and Kusang played cards. 'OK, you can come in now,' he finally conceded. Bemused by his actions we stood back and watched him dig his karmic grave.

Not only did we not want to rope up with Kusang but his very presence at Base Camp clearly undermined the success of the entire trip. Rather than be passive victims of his tyranny, we decided to fire him. The next morning we called Bishnu, our liaison officer, into the tent and went over the record-keeping step by step. He was in agreement with our conclusions, but feared Sangay and Sanglai would likely follow Kusang, leaving poor Bishnu alone. My whole body shook in fear and apprehension of the ugly scene that I anticipated the following day. The conflicts of K2 were still raw and open in my mind. Why was this happening to us?

By morning, calmness and deliberation prevailed. We went into the mess tent and Chris sat down and calmly repeated what we had gone over with Bishnu. Kusang offered no real defence except, 'You ask other sardars — they tell you food very expensive here.' Then, like a loaded gun he shot out, 'OK, if one bad we all bad. Come Sangay, Sanglai, we go.' Chris was ready for it and quickly intervened by telling Sangay and Sanglai that as individuals they were free to make up their own minds. Chris took Sanglai aside and said, 'You stay?' With a quiet voice and lowered eyes he replied, 'OK.' From that point on our trip was saved. It was a gigantic moral victory.

Torn between traditional loyalties to his countrymen and the inner loyalties toward his Buddhist principals of correct action, Sanglai's choice could have made him an unpopular figure with his peers in Kathmandu. Yet as a Tamang he was considered an outsider in any event, trying to encroach on the exclusive and highly lucrative domain of Himalayan mountaineering that Sherpas as a race had enjoyed since the beginning of climbing in Nepal. A humble Tamang kitchen boy was acceptable, but hardworking Sherpa kitchen boys had a habit of patiently working their way up through the ranks to become high altitude porters and eventually sardars. Yet this route of upward mobility was usually blocked to a Tamang. His sharp mind was quick to see a career opportunity. We were glad to give it to him, although I felt instinctively that his actions were based ultimately on what he considered to be fair and just, rather than on self-interest.

Sangay on the other hand was having great difficulty with the decision. Although not exactly thrilled by his performance, we felt that away from Kusang, he would improve. We wanted to start out with a clean slate and encouraged him to consider his career. There was a brief exchange between Kusang and Sangay, then Sangay nodded his consent, yes, he would stay with the trip. A mood of co-operation took an unsteady lead when we agreed to write a letter at Kusang's request, giving medical reasons for his dismissal. He even admitted his mistakes and stated a willingness to learn from the experience. As he was no longer sardar we wished him to leave behind one of the two sleeping bags he was issued, as Sanglai's sleeping bag had seen better feathers. He would be adequately reimbursed in rupees. The avariciousness we had seen in the past loomed again — nothing really had changed. He failed to recognise the generous concessions we had extended and would concede to nothing. Perhaps he thought he could get a better price for the sleeping bag from some poor trekker in Kathmandu. Co-operation took a fall and landed on the rocks, never to recover. We tore up the letter and wrote to Mike Cheney about the real reasons for Kusang's dismissal. Kusang left, a lone figure descending in an approaching snowstorm, heavily laden with all the material things he could carry. I suspected his heart had an even heavier load.

We went though the supplies, making a careful inventory to

figure out how much more food would be needed. We cut out the mail run to Tapeljung for the purchase of candles, as kerosene lanterns would do. In the process, a 1,500 rupees shopping list was culled to 300 rupees. Sangay handed Chris 60 rupees, the first change we had seen the entire trip. A feeling of control replaced the frustration that had been growing since the beginning. Why had we waited so long to take decisive action? Chris's method of dealing with people was by appealing to the higher levels of human motivation — he believed that respecting the god that lay within others would sharpen their awareness of those qualities that bring about good service. He wanted to be certain beyond all doubt that Kusang would not work out. In fact, by the time of Kusang's dismissal, it appeared he was actively sabotaging the trip.

Kusang's departure had lifted a giant weight off our shoulders, but the cost was telling. Feeling drained from the combined effects of the confrontation and the altitude, we lay about Base Camp in a state of inertia. Like flies that had strayed too far into the honey-pot, we floundered. The classic rib which cut directly up the north face to the summit pyramid of Yalung Kang waited patiently.

Frequent avalanches off Wedge Peak continued into the night, disturbing the peace my mind sought. Sleep was fitful. It did not help that the only approach to the base of our rib seemed desperately dangerous, guarded by monstrous hanging walls of ice.

After a leisurely breakfast we took off at about 10 am, with nothing more than light lunch packs. To gain access to the glacier, it was necessary to drop down about 150 m (500 ft) to a jumble of large boulders that covered the lower section. I was soon to be reminded of the relative newness of the Himalayas. If you stepped on one rock and it moved, it would be likely that ten more would follow. We played a dancing game, skipping between the rolling boulders. It was an entertaining exercise, but one did have to be careful; a friend of Chris's had his back severely crushed by playing such a game.

Two options appeared open. Either to follow a direct route down the centre of the glacier, the one Dyrenfurth and his team had chosen in 1930, or to opt for hugging the eastern side, the choice of Doug Scott's group. Cairns that led through the initial section now petered out. We tried moving directly into the centre but it proved totally impractical. We would constantly be making detours because of steep impassable gullies, glazed ridges and pinnacles of ice. Forget it. We hung a left to find ourselves floundering in thigh-deep snow. 'Joy of joys', we sarcastically commented back and forth to each other. Such conditions are a familiar, but always unwelcome experience in Himalayan climbing. There was only one consolation in sticking with the eastern route. Providing there wasn't a heavy snowfall every day, once the route was through it would be considerably easier with each load carry. We turned back to Base Camp.

It was on the way back to Pang Pema, when I was feeling rather tired from the day's exertions, that Chris mentioned he thought I should cut higher on the moraine. I could quite clearly see the cairn, a pile of rocks used as a marker, and the one further on, and so felt perfectly comfortable at the angle I was approaching. I decided simply to continue as I had been doing. By the third time he told me, there was definite tension in the air. I felt he was imposing a decision on me that made little difference one way or the other. 'I know he is a better climber than me, but this is bullshit,' I thought to myself. I was now involved with what was going on between the two of us instead of what was around me, and a rock rolled on my leg. Fortunately no harm was done. It was a slow roll, but my reaction was to snap, 'Look, if you want to go that way it's fine with me. I'm happy where I'm at.'

Chris ripped off his $80 sunglasses and smashed them into the rocks, yelling that I was destroying the love between us by my constant criticism — he felt stifled by it and had given up all hope. I was terrified by the outburst of anger and the depth of his emotions, though it scarcely made sense to me. My instinct was to run away as far as I could and find some place to hide. I took off like a scared rabbit but stopped suddenly, dead in my tracks. A strange voice I didn't even recognise as Chris's croaked, 'Help me please, Cherie.' Just as his anger cut me to the very marrow, so did his plea. An indescribable feeling filled the air as our souls touched. I swung around to see him standing there, head lowered. Reaching out to embrace him I was overwhelmed by the paradox: one moment I faced a terrifying vacuum and moments later an enormous release, a letting go. Somehow the sunglasses didn't matter, the mountain didn't matter. All that mattered was that we were together.

In talking over the responses we had both had to each other's actions, I admitted that even if he had made an unnecessary comment, my criticism of it caused far greater harm than a lighthearted shrug of the shoulder. Purged by the experience we drew closer in love and understanding than ever before. How could we hold onto it? Crying softly to myself, I tried to put the sunglasses back together again. They could not be mended.

Over the following week, with Sanglai's help, we ferried loads to Camp 1. Close to 5,500 m (18,500 ft), it was tenuously located between avalanches and rock falls from the Twins, Gimmigela I and II at over 7,000 m (23,000 ft) on one side, and the towering seracs of Kangbachen 7,903 m (25,928 ft) on the other. It was like being on a firing range and we were the targets. We were well aware that the highest incidence of death in the Himalayas was by avalanche, and that it was most likely to occur when the climbers were snuggled warmly in their tents at night. It was in the tent that most time, by necessity, was spent. Choosing a campsite, therefore, required the utmost care and in order to make the optimum choice, one had to free oneself from ego, fears and anxieties, and achieve inner quiet.

Sanglai's help over the previous four days had proved to be a great moral boost — equipped with a pair of my double boots it did not seem to matter at all to him that he was running over moraine in large cumbersome footware designed for 7,800 m (26,000 ft). Chris recounted to me a story of one of the mail runners on his Everest trip who also wore double boots, but over terrain where tennis shoes would have sufficed. To make matters worse, he had some years earlier suffered a severe break of his lower leg, just above the ankle. It had healed out of alignment. The result was a gross deformity of jutting bone which must have been rubbed horribly by the rigid boots. Nonetheless the fellow performed his duties with cheerfulness and zeal. Chris's entreaties to the poor man to change his footwear proved to no avail. It seems the boots were a highly prized status symbol.

Crampons, ice axe, harness, down pants and vest, plus a good carrying pack were added to Sanglai's equipment. He was rapidly acquiring all the paraphernalia of a bona fide climber. He giggled with joy at each new item. Then we gave him a salary increase to equal Kusang's. His childlike nature and innocence were delightfully endearing. Sincerity, freedom from any hint of greed or cunning was a balm to heal the wound of the Kusang association. Despite his openness, Sanglai also had the capacity to plunge into unfathomable seriousness — giving the appearance of uncanny wisdom for his years. It was too bad the language barrier didn't allow us to probe his mind further. By the end of the trip we were so indebted to this dear person who had given us so much of himself, that we literally gave him the shirts off our backs. That mattered little to him. Such is the nature of some people.

With the onset of bad weather, Sanglai was forced to return to Base Camp while we chose to stay at Camp 1 for rest and recuperation. We would get to test the wisdom of our campsite choice. Rest days are generally grand affairs, especially with the most wonderful of excuses, BAD WEATHER, to eliminate any lingering shadows of guilt about not making just *one* more carry. Strictly speaking, we should have returned to Base Camp to conserve supplies, but we desired the luxury of total isolation. It would also put us in a good position to push the route through the first icefall should a break in weather occur unexpectedly, as well as aid us in the gradual acclimatisation process.

Listening to the music of Muddy Waters, Nina Simone and other old favourites, we made endless cups of hot chocolate laced with a preciously small cache of run. 'Drink plenty of fluids now, can't afford to get dehydrated.' Chris fussed around me. I took the doctor's advice. We indulged our tastebuds with culinary delights such as fresh yak butter and garlic, adding to our diet of prepackaged minute rice and dehydrated vegies. Such simple things provided boundless comfort. Making love was so gentle, yet so sensuous, a stark contrast to the formidable environment we were separated from by the thin fabric of the tent. Chris read to me for hours from *Tales of Power* by Carlos Castaneda. The snow outside fell lightly but persistently. I really liked what Don Juan said about power. In order to have power one must be impeccable with one's inner core of values; one must not look to others for approval or disapproval. I thought about how being in love would allow for

AERIAL VIEW OF KANCHENJUNGA

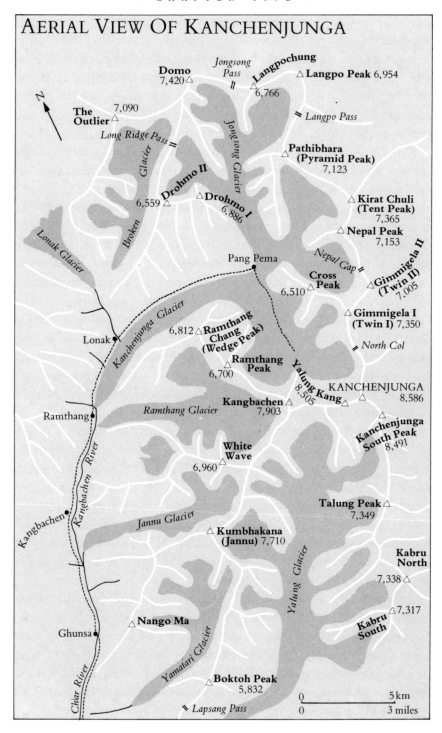

Jongsong Pass
Domo 7,420 △

Langpochung 6,766 △

△ **Langpo Peak** 6,954

The Outlier 7,090 △

= *Langpo Pass*

Long Ridge Pass =

Jongsong Glacier

△ **Pathibhara (Pyramid Peak)** 7,123

Broken Glacier

Drohmo II 6,559 △

△ **Drohmo I** 6,886

△ **Kirat Chuli (Tent Peak)** 7,365

△ **Nepal Peak** 7,153

Lonak Glacier

Nepal Gap =

△ **Gimmigela II (Twin II)** 7,005

Pang Pema •

Cross Peak 6,510 △

△ **Gimmigela I (Twin I)** 7,350

Kanchenjunga Glacier

6,812 △ **Ramthang Chang (Wedge Peak)**

Yalung Kang 8,505

= *North Col*

Lonak •

Ramthang Peak 6,700 △

KANCHENJUNGA 8,586

Ramthang •

Ramthang Glacier

Kangbachen 7,903 △

△ Yalung Kang △

Kangbachen River

White Wave 6,960 △

Kanchenjunga South Peak 8,491

Jannu Glacier

Talung Peak △ 7,349

Kangbachen •

△ **Kumbhakana (Jannu)** 7,710

Yalung Glacier

Kabru North 7,338 △

△ 7,317

△ **Nango Ma**

Kabru South

Ghunsa •

Yamatari Glacier

Chiar River

△ **Boktoh Peak** 5,832

\\ *Lapsang Pass*

| 0 | | 5 km |
| 0 | | 3 miles |

this, and it was a tough one for me. I had to admit that generally I thought of myself as a cynic, quick to see through the often self-glorifying mumbo-jumbo ramblings of self-proclaimed psychics and their gullible herd of followers. What I did enjoy from the writings, fact or fiction, was Castaneda's way of getting the reader to stretch the stiff old mind out of its rigid programming and self-imposed limits, to reach out and contemplate the impossible.

Rambling thoughts wandered into late afternoon, punctuated by missiles of flying rock from behind and occasional small avalanches that came off Kangbachen in explosions of white smoke, like a magician performing tricks. Nodding off into a happy dream world, I was shaken into awareness by a deep resounding thud. The ground quivered. A loud roar filled the air. We both sprang to attention and peered out of the tent door. 'Oh shit, this is a big one,' Chris groaned. We watched, mesmerised, as tons of ice came toppling down. It was as though the film had been turned to slow motion. As one block of ice peeled off, another and yet another followed in endless succession. Hundreds of tons fell to the glacier floor, several thousand feet below, pulverising everything in its path. Stored energy ran rampant towards us, once released. We held on to the tent frames to brace ourselves as the full fury of the onslaught hit moments later.

Sharp needles of ice blasted the fabric of the tent, through multiple layers of clothes, to the skin, and we rocked under the initial impact. Tingling pain, then, 'Ouch!', I yelled. A pellet that felt as large as a golf ball had just hit my back. I wondered if anything larger were to follow. Finally it was over. Everything in the tent had been covered by a thin film of powdered ice. We went outside and shook ourselves, laughing nervously. A large block of ice lying about 30 m (100 ft) from our tent had been defeated by a small rise in the glacier. We had been lucky.

This incident confirmed our decision once and for all that the most direct route to the rib, traversing under the icefall of Kangbachen, meant taking unnecessary risks. We would turn the easterly bend in the glacier to reach an altitude of about 6,000 m (20,000 ft) and look at other possibilities for gaining the first snow terrace. This would be making a large zig zag in our route, but hopefully we would be less open to such dangerous avalanches.

We plodded on. I wrote in my diary: 'Camp 2 established April 17. We've got 22 days low altitude food and 12 days high altitude, plus 28 gas cylinders for cooking. With the soul-destroying task of breaking trail through this deep snow, plus putting in the route through the first icefall, we figure it will take another 10 days before Camp 3 is established.'

Our food had been organised, prepacked and weighed in Seattle. The low altitude food (to be consumed up to 7,000 m/23,000 ft) consisted of breakfast of powdered eggs flavoured with Parmesan cheese and crackers; lunch of mixed nuts and dried fruit, cheese crackers and a can of oysters or sardines; and dinner of either noodles and cheese or tuna, or quick brown rice spiced up with ginger, garlic and mushrooms or shrimp. High calorie breakfast drinks — hot chocolates, soups and teas — made up our beverages, which we consumed in large quantities. The simplicity and mono-tony of the diet didn't particularly bother us. We could always fantasise.

We had both experienced the exorbitant cost and other draw-backs of commercial freeze-dried food: the body seemed to crave calories no matter how much was eaten. It was as though the body could not assimilate the food offered, probably in part due to the gut's lowered oxygen supply, and in part to the freeze-dried food itself. Large bulky stools, often with pieces of undigested carrot and pea clearly visible, seemed to confirm the feeling. Our diet, though simple, lacking variety and heavier in weight, did not produce these effects. The nuts and dried fruit were the hardest to digest. They produced an annoying diarrhoea, and were often left uneaten or sometimes cooked as a dessert at night. The high altitude food was primarily liquid. Prepackaged 'smoothies' — a recipe of powdered milk, egg, protein mix and lecithin, flavoured with nutmeg and cinnamon — provided a nutritious and easily prepared drink by simply adding hot water. The usual soups, hot chocolates and teas were included. Coffee made me feel nauseous.

The low altitude food packs were designed to feed two people for one day and weighed 2 kg (4 lb) — similar high altitude packs weighed 1 kg (2 lb). Each had the advantage that they could be easily spun out over several days, should the need arise. We liked the system as we could easily estimate how much weight we were carrying, especially since all equipment, down to the last karabiner, had been weighed beforehand.

One of the most interesting discoveries came from the inclusion of controversial daily megadoses of vitamins B, C and E in my diet. In the past I had always been troubled by herpes simplex (cold sores). This is a rather common, but benign complaint. However, the combination of constant exposure to ultraviolet light (despite the fanatical use of sunblocks), wind, cold and stress can turn what is ordinarily a simple annoyance into a real problem. I had been so severely affected on Dhaulagiri that at night my lips glued together from the raw open lesions. Opening my mouth in the morning to take a sip of water was excruciatingly painful — gums, tongue, the roof of my mouth and throat were all covered with the lesions. It made chewing and swallowing difficult. On K2 I'd offered myself as a guinea pig to try out some experimental medication, taken as hypodermic injections every three weeks. That had helped to keep the condition under control; it only broke out in a fresh lesion if I was due for the medication. When I returned to civilisation however, without the medication, the sores broke out in an angry beard over my chin, mouth and nose. With the inclusion of megavitamins in my diet I was completely free from the problem for the entire trip. I was elated. I realised it was far from a scientific study, but I had found relief and that was all that mattered.

Sanglai had left us after helping ferry loads to a dump site about 150 m (500 ft) below our actual Camp 2. It had been clear that he was uncomfortable crossing the deep unconsolidated snow that covered hidden crevasses, seemingly in every direction. The Japanese had used a 9 m (30 ft) steel ladder to cover a section we found ourselves swimming through. I had not liked it one bit, so understood well enough when we asked Sanglai why he was descending: 'Too cold? Don't like food? Don't like work?' and the only thing he said was, 'I only small boy.' We were grateful for the help he had given and reluctantly said goodbye.

During this period of the trip my diary is full of the fights that occurred with Chris. Writing became a safe form of emotional release. The topic was too painful for either of us to be able to discuss it openly. I needed to straighten things out in my mind, to get some grasp on why it was happening. Writing it down seemed to make it more real. After a while, I just wanted to blot it out and forget it even happened, so I stopped writing. What I could not stop was the internal dialogue, etching the events slowly and persistently into my mind.

I had reached the chilling realisation that Chris's outbursts had little to do with what I did or how I did it. Just as the inherent stresses of an icefall reach a critical limit then unpredictably release their load of chaotic violence, so Chris needed a release. Unfortunately I was usually in the path. Rather than fight back with a force I was incapable of matching, I gave in to it. I hung on to the sunglasses incident like a lifeline. How effortlessly we had cut through the layers of garbage then to find one another. Though scarcely in control of the situation, we rode out the storms as they came, and focused on the beauty and calm that followed.

One night, unable to sleep, I slipped quietly outside and without a thread of clothing, sat on a rock under the glow of the full moon. Trailing a thousand and one silken scarves in exotic dance, the wind and mountain met. It was breathtakingly beautiful and I quickly fell into a deep contemplative state. In spite of it being early spring it must have been fairly cold at over 6,000 m (20,000 ft), yet in a state of deep relaxation I was warm, having let go of all my cares. Although untrained in higher yogic practices, I never came close to getting frostbite or hypothermia. Thoughts rolled back to Dhaulagiri when, at 6,000 m (20,000 ft) on the north col, Terry had fallen into a crevasse. His pack had become wedged and he was forced to leave it behind. He barely managed to extricate himself from the crevasse's jaws and was deeply chilled by the hours of effort involved in getting out. I gave him my down jacket to prevent a deadly hypothermia setting in. As he was on one side of the crevasse and I was on the other, we were unable to combine our bodily warmth to survive the bivouac. I was left with a thin woollen shirt and windbreaker and was happily surprised that, by practising breath control, I felt little cold. It seemed bodily warmth had more to do with controlling energy flows than ambient temperature and layers of clothing. The hypothermic state I'd found myself in on K2 was probably a result of energy dispersal rather than any other factor.

Much later I learnt the mechanism of bio-feedback. The scientist's measurement of alpha waves on an electro-encepholgram is the characteristic brainwave pattern produced when someone meditates. This in turn produces a vasodilatory effect — in other words, the blood vessels to the extremities dilate, producing warmth which helps to prevent chilling and frostbite.

Alexandra David-Neel in her book *Magic and Mystery in Tibet* describes two methods of 'warming oneself without fire in the snows'. *Tumo* (warming) is produced by effecting a deep hypnotic state, visualising the blood vessels filled with fire, and breath control. The other method of *tumo* is achieved by churning the stomach from left to right three times, shaking the body 'as a restive horse shakes himself' and performing a short leap whilst keeping the legs in a crossed position. These calisthenics should be performed three times in succession then concluded with a leap, jumping as high as possible. David-Neel notes, 'It does not appear very wonderful to me that a man should feel warm after performing this feat.' Apparently this method was borrowed from Indian hatha yoga practices and is unconnected with true *tumo*, the deep hypnotic state practised by Tibetans, for which she apparently has the utmost respect.

David-Neel goes on to describe a kind of competition that is sometimes held on frosty winter nights beside a lake or river. Neophytes sit cross-legged on the ground. They are wrapped in sheets that have been dipped in the icy waters. If the water is frozen over, then a hole is made through the ice. Whoever dries the largest number of sheets by their body heat is the winner! Chris apparently thought I had a way to go. On discovering me missing, he had come looking and found me sitting on the rock, naked. Deaf to my protests, he dragged me back into the tent.

It was time for a rest and with a break in the weather we decided to return to Base Camp. The day before we had been surprised by an enormous avalanche that swept over our proposed route and the entire rib. We had anticipated the route to be relatively free of danger. It looked as if the ice cliffs to the right would clear the rib; instead they had wiped it clean. Rather than be exposed to danger for a relatively short period of time in the process of gaining access to the rib, the whole route would be under constant threat. This was unacceptable to us, so we opted for the 'Japanese route'.

Though it looked somewhat formidable, it had shown remarkably little activity in the way of avalanches. It was a good thing our plans were fluid! We would now try to tackle Yalung Kang from the 7,800 m (26,000 ft) level. We hoped to gain access to the summit pyramid from the east. From our present elevation of 6,000 m (20,000 ft), this route appeared to have some temptingly easy snow gullies that would lead us to the top. The paucity of information we had been able to glean from other expeditions left a big question mark in our minds, and kept the excitement level high. What would we find? Would it be plausible?

On return to Pang Pema we received news from Sanglai who had just returned from a mail run to Ghunsa that we would no longer have the mountain to ourselves. A Czechoslovakian group of 15 climbers, one sardar and one liaison officer would be sharing the same route to 7,800 m (26,000 ft). Above that, they would continue to the main summit while we would look at the options on Yalung Kang.

We were taken by surprise. The news bitterly disappointed us. For one, the isolation we so cherished would be broken. For another, despite the fact that we were a full two weeks ahead in fitness and acclimatisation, such a large group would probably overtake us and we would end up climbing in their footsteps. A race to keep ahead of them was not exactly what we had in mind. We tried to counter the depressing news by reminding ourselves that their presence on the mountain could keep the descent route open, providing a considerable safety factor.

About two hours later the Czech team started popping their heads through the cook tent door. Being such open friendly people, it was impossible to feel anything but genuine warmth in return, despite our disappointment and sudden change of thinking. Bishnu was clearly delighted to have a fellow police officer to chat with. He had obviously felt the isolation most acutely, giving up his own tent and caste restrictions to sleep in the cook tent, huddling beside Sangay and Sanglai. All three openly admitted to hearing strange noises at night, believing that in our absence the camp had been stalked by a yeti, ghost or even both.

The Czechs' presence at Base Camp changed the whole atmosphere — and it was not for the worse. Over the following evenings we developed friendships with some of the English-speaking members of the group. Coming from an Eastern Bloc country, there were unending lively discussions and comparisons to be made. They had taken the long journey overland from Czechoslovakia in several trucks carrying all their food and equipment. There had been much difficulty with breakdowns and customs duties that had to be paid in US dollars. It seemed a miracle they were even here.

Foreign currency was exceedingly difficult to obtain so everything possible was brought from home, including all food. Our eyes boggled at the big heavy cans, wonderful sausages, cheeses and breads. It was a good thing they were a strong healthy bunch, their packs would weigh twice our own! Russia had just invaded Afghanistan and they were clearly preoccupied with thoughts of returning to their homeland to be drafted and sent off to fight a war against a people they felt no animosity towards, and for a master they clearly resented, Russia. We surmised that if Reagan were to declare war against the Russians, we would find ourselves facing combat with our newfound friends. These power struggles of nations seemed so absurd. The news that Reagan had been shot was picked up by the BBC broadcast on our tiny radio. I imagined world headlines and the flurry of TV cameramen, hot for the latest dramatic event. It all had such a different perspective here. No wonder I always returned to civilisation with a peculiar reluctance.

Refreshed in body and spirit we roused ourselves from a deep slumber at three the next morning, and by four found ourselves stumbling across the boulders and moraine in the light of the fading moon and early approach of dawn. Reaching Camp 1 about 7 am, it was still too cold even to sip on the water we were carrying. It left my mouth numb. Somehow we managed to stuff the dry chapattis (unleavened bread) down our parched throats and munch on boiled eggs that had frozen in the early morning cold. It was stimulating to see what our bodies were capable of, and how well we had responded to the rest at lower elevation. We arrived back at Camp 2 at 11.30 am. I reflected on the effort it had taken previously to reach the same point, even without the heavy loads we had just

We traverse a broad snow and ice field to join the north ridge at approximately 7,200 m (24,000 ft). (Photo Chris Chandler)

carried. Such are the wonders of acclimatisation to altitude; the myriad microscopic adjustments the body makes to less oxygen and lowered atmospheric pressure.

All our attention was now riveted on the easternmost section of the first icefall. An ice gully briefly caught our eyes, polished and shining bright by the passage of tons of ice. Though obviously not free of danger, the icefall appeared technically straightforward for a distance of 90−120 m (300−400 ft), before it broke up into shorter vertical sections and wound westwards to the eventual safety of the first great snow terrace. We wondered how quickly we could move through this section. This was the most dangerous part of the mountain for avalanche risk. We either had to accept the fact that we could be annihilated at any moment while climbing it, or turn around and go home. The worst of the avalanche debris was to the right of our route, but that gave little comfort. I wrote in my diary that night: 'Quest for tomorrow — direct anxieties into positive action. Action dispels and allays fear. Approach our goal one step at a time. Look at each step behind us with satisfaction. Only look at the whole in order to plan the sequential steps, don't remain fixed on it. Otherwise it will paralyse us.'

The day before, a seven-hour carry had been cut short at 11.30 am. We had not wanted to tire ourselves out for the following day, anticipating that with light loads we would just zip right over to the icefall and start putting up the route. It was not to be so. Acclimatised as we were to 6,000 (20,000 ft) it seemed as if we were one foot higher. We plummeted back to our snail-like progress. Making headway through the thigh deep snow and maze of crevasses was made easier for me by switching leads, but did little for Chris who would often fall through my steps. Slowly we inched our way into the shadow of the icefall, picking our way through the icy tomb-stones of avalanche debris. The massive broken blocks emphasised just how fully we had surrendered ourselves to fate.

The sun was now high in the sky. A slight tinkling of ice as a small crystal melted in the heat and broke off, attuned and livened

A snow cave on the north ridge is built with a drinking cup and snowfluke. (Our shovel had been buried in an ice avalanche.) The snow cave provided us with insulation from the cold as well as shelter from the high winds. Peaks of Sikkim poke through thick cloud cover below. (Photo Chris Chandler)

the senses. Instincts on edge, we were as alive as stalked animals, waiting for the hunter to make his move. This was not a blind panic, we were not frozen in fear, but experiencing a deep sense of inner calm, facing the invincible flow of karma.

Now we were across the bergschrund that marked the beginning of the gully and the first climbing of any real difficulty began. Chris led off, his crampons skipping over the hard water ice before biting. It was hard climbing, but with the skill and confidence that was the result of years of experience, he proceeded upwards in quick, easy movements. I loved to watch him, and relaxed a little; it was good to be thinking about something other than impending doom.

No sense in dilly-dallying. Sixty metres (200 ft) up, with ice screws and pickets securing the line in place, we rappelled back down in falling snow with a satisfaction that we had not felt in weeks, and made our way back to camp. Over several days the route was fixed with 90 m (300 ft) of line. We could have used more but elected to save it for higher up the mountain. Climbing on the ice had been fun. Camp 3, a small one-person hut, was established on 29 April at about 6,750 m (22,500 ft). This was not as high as we would have liked, but seemed about the maximum height we could expect to carry a load to in the deep snow from Camp 2. There had been snowfall each afternoon and we had been forced to break a new trail every day. This situation had coerced us into using a dump site at the base of the icefall. In better conditions we planned to ferry the loads quickly through the icefall to Camp 3.

After one month on the mountain the course of our trip was dramatically altered. The Czechs were now abreast of us, and after some debate amongst themselves had elected to use the fixed lines we already had in place. It was interesting to observe the mental adjustments they were making in order to come to terms with accepting and dealing with the risks of the route; just the same mental gymnastics we had gone through weeks earlier. Now we were all hooked as the mountain drew us closer. The Czechs' Camp 2 was established in the middle of the glacier — we thought somewhat uncomfortably close to the ice cliffs.

During the night the ground shook with an avalanche. I knew it had been a big one and we wondered about the Czech camp. Morning revealed the activity of an ants' nest. Fortunately, the Czechs' camp was only blasted, but some of their cached supplies had been buried. They decided to move location. Regrettably, all our carefully packed food, fuel, fixed line and hardware for the upper mountain had also been buried under tons of ice. Our reaction was a curious mixture of relief and dismay. Thank God it was not people — too bad about all our gear being buried! This certainly ensured we would be a lightweight expedition. We returned to Base Camp and re-evaluated the situation.

At Pang Pema, spare crampon parts of several makes were assembled and pronounced inadequate but probably usable. Eggs, broken raw in quart polybottles, and chapattis were added to the spartan six days food rations. The Czechs graciously gave us 16 gas cylinder cartridges which would help tremendously. Our bivvy sac was gone, along with the shovel. We would improvise with a snowfluke and drinking cup for digging snow caves. As no fixed line or rock gear was left and very little ice gear remained, our options were getting quite small. We decided to be a bit extreme and left one of our two Gortex-covered half sacs behind to save on weight. We had made them ourselves, they were stuffed with extra down and covered with heavyweight Gortex. Warm but heavy. We would rather cram two bodies into one half sac. It was a good thing we liked one another! The ingredients of a summit attempt slowly took shape.

On 6 May we re-ascended the 1,500 vertical metres (5,000 ft) to Camp 3. The next day we discovered that the snow terrace, which was so attractively free from hanging cliffs, had another problem. Snow that had trickled and sifted down from the cliffs above, with snow blown from the upper part of the mountain, had caused unconsolidated waist-deep snow to accumulate on the 15–30 degree slopes. A cold wind had hardened the upper surface. It was prime slab avalanche country.

The lightning pace of yesterday's assent was brought to a grinding halt as we broke through the hard surface using our shoulders to ram a pathway, creating almost a tunnel through the deepest sections. My patience was running out. With 25 kg (50 lb) packs, I thought the situation outrageous. I was just plain sick of it. I sat down to contemplate a strike. Chris was being mellow and suggested we just take a good break instead. Although close to 7,000 m (23,000 ft) it was quite hot and we sat back in the snow and drank Tang, munched on crackers and smoked oysters, and looked out over the Tibetan plateau. God it was so beautiful. I started to feel better. We could even pick out Everest and Makalu 160 km (100 miles) away.

Suddenly, we were surrounded by a strange noise, like the sound of someone being kicked in the stomach. A forceful escapement of air preceding a groan. The ground shook. My insides contracted at the thought of an avalanche. We sprang up, looking around for the source, to see about 200 square metres of glacier settle down about 2 m (6 ft), like a blanket that had just been fluffed. The interior of the glacier had undergone an entire resettlement plan. One of the crevasses was still puffing out a telltale plume of smoke. We had been sitting on the perimeter of the event.

Stimulated more by adrenalin than enthusiasm, we continued on in these dreadful conditions to locate a crevasse at about 7,000 m (23,000 ft), just below the rock band. We aptly named it the 'bookshelf bivvy'. Remarkable for its lack of headroom and with one side missing, we felt like two books sitting on a bookshelf. The setting sun created a spectacular view. Bathed in gold and red we set up house and, during dinner preparations, discussed a hot topic: how on earth does Messner do it? Acclaimed as the world's greatest Himalayan climber, he has climbed a number of peaks higher than 8,000 m (27,000 ft) solo, including Mount Everest without oxygen.

We thought it prudent to take a rest day at the new elevation and recover from the tortures of the day before. We sat back and watched the Czechs follow in our hard-won trail to set up camp just below ours. We now faced a pretty hard decision: should we follow behind the Czechs who obviously wanted to lead the 360 m (1,200 ft) mixed ice and rock band that was above us? Taking advantage of their numbers and equipment would certainly make things easier for us. But instead we decided to jeopardise our chances of success by climbing the mountain ourselves, in the style we wanted, or not climb it at all.

Our eyes traced a line that followed a 50 degree snow and ice slope, previously unclimbed, that led to the north ridge. This was taking us even further from our objective of Yalung Kang, but was attractive in that it would not require fixing with rope because it was easier than the rock band and its shining surface indicated ice. We would be leaving the floundering snowdrifts behind. Pondering on Messner's tactics we decided to lighten our loads even further. So out went a few ice screws, karabiners and our extra rope. With a sense of relief at solving the two problems of the Czechs and our equipment in a single move, we took off and climbed to about 30 m (100 ft) below the ridge. Here, among some boulders and drifted snow, we found an ideal preconstructed cave. It even had a nice air vent overhead.

The winds above roared over the ridge, but we felt protected in our shelter and settled down, enjoying the starry night through our skylight. At some stage during the night the wind direction changed, and instead of being protected we found ourselves in the full force of 80-knot winds. We clutched one another for warmth. This was not much fun. It was now obvious how our skylight had been formed. We were directly in the path of winds that collected in such a way they channelled combined forces to spit out of the top of the cave. The 'blowhole bivvy' was not one of our favourite places.

By morning we had taken on the appearance of verglased scarecrows, our hair standing out vertically in frozen fright. The weak warmth from the sun was just sufficient to thaw our stiffened bodies and dry out our clothing. We spent several hours digging a proper cave on the crest of the ridge itself. By the time it was complete a full gale was blowing and we climbed gratefully inside to warmth and safety.

We were now about 7,300 m (24,300 ft) and starting to feel the sluggish effects of altitude. It was important to rehydrate and we kept the stove going, providing an almost endless round of soup, hot chocolate and tea. With the stove balanced on my lap, I started to nod off to sleep. A sudden jerk startled me awake. I almost spilt the soup. I opened my mouth to speak but instead, a slurred jumble of unintelligible sounds fell out of the side of my drooped mouth. My heart began to race. What was happening to me — a stroke at 7,200 m (24,000 ft)? As suddenly as it had happened, my words became clear and my mouth normal again. I laughed nervously.

'That was a close one. Just stick me in a crevasse and leave me there if it happens again and I don't come out of it. It's the only way,' I told Chris. 'Don't worry sweetheart, I'd find a way to get you down. I'd never leave you,' he answered quietly. We went ahead and enlarged the hole we'd constructed for ventilation and placed the stove at the cave entrance.

Sleep really didn't qualify as such, but was more a series of catnaps and sudden jerks into consciousness with the realisation that I had forgotten to breathe. I was experiencing the phenomenon of Cheyne-Stokes breathing, where the respirations gradually become shallower and shallower until they cease altogether. The person finally realises something is not right and is stimulated by panic to take another breath, only for the cycle to be repeated. It is a familiar and universal condition at high altitude.

Another physiological adjustment is an increase in red blood cells in response to low oxygen. The blood thickens to such an extent that scientific expeditions report difficulties in drawing samples. The blood clots like jelly either in the needle or in the syringe, before it can be transferred to a vial. The combination of thickened blood, inactivity enforced by bad weather and dehydration caused by the excessively dry atmosphere makes blood clots a common occurrence in the high altitude climber.

When the blood supply is suddenly interrupted to the organ or tissue that it is supplying — be it a leg, part of a lung, heart or brain — death of that part will inevitably occur. My 'cerebral event' was a warning of dangerously sluggish circulation. I was fortunate that it was transient. Not only was there danger without, but it lay within ourselves as well.

We started out early the next morning, moving through light powder snow in conditions so frigid my feet lost feeling almost immediately. With heavy down mitts and several layers of gloves underneath, it was even hard to keep my hands from losing sensation as well. Though unable to feel anything from the knees down, I consciously attempted to wiggle my toes to get the circulation moving. I hoped they were doing as they were told. With the exertion of climbing, I was counting on everything warming up more.

To our left, Sikkim sat beneath a heavy blanket of cloud.

To the right, Pang Pema and a distant green valley lay 1,800 m (6,000 ft) below in a different world. Rising steeply before us, a rock buttress about 180 m (600 ft) high dubbed 'the castle' by Doug Scott's group, lay between us and the great scree and snow terrace above. Fortunately for us, with our lack of rock-climbing equipment, a tongue of snow that turned into steep ice led to a weakness in the barrier. It was there the rocky fortress dropped its guard to allow a 15 m (50 ft) step onto the snow and scree terrace above. With our combined energies directed to that weakness, we took turns leading through the deep avalanche-prone slopes that dropped disconcertingly thousands of feet into Sikkim.

Persistent westerlies blew snow from the slopes above. The snow funnelled and trickled its way through the rocky crevices to collect in large unconsolidated layers, as we had found on the slopes below. Anchoring ourselves for protection with 'dead-men' — a piece of equipment used for deep snow conditions — seemed a waste of time and we held our breath in suspense. My feet by now had thawed, but the thought that at least my big toes might still be frozen was worrisome. The brilliantly clear day we had started out with now showed a giant halo around the sun. A certain harbinger of bad weather. The wind above us was gaining in velocity, whipping off 'the castle' and streaming in a long tail towards Tibet. In no time at all it had dropped to where we were standing. By 10.30 am we found ourselves with zero visibility and in the middle of a major storm.

Out came the snowfluke and drinking cup, and taking advantage of a conveniently located crevasse, we enlarged its roof, nailed down a few missing floorboards, cleaned out the cobwebs in the corners and hey presto, home! But where was the wood for a cosy fire? Striking a match didn't quite do it, but did produce a weak blue flame from the stove. The warm fluid sent a glow through our chilled bodies and we snuggled next to one another, resigned to a long and uneasy vigil. We were now unable to go up or down. Little remained of our food and fuel. Wasted leg muscles and bony rib cages revealed that the gruelling work of the past weeks had far surpassed our calorie intake. What if the storm lasted a week or even longer? How many times can you wring out a teabag? We began to practise. 'If you're not supposed to feel hungry at high altitude, how come I feel I could eat a horse?' I complained to Chris. 'That's a good sign,' he replied in his most professional manner. Who was fooling who, anyway?

To overcome the dread and loathing that seems to be the hallmark of hypoxia, I discovered a marvellous panacea: sexual fantasies that I'd had a boob job done and was an absolute knockout. No man could resist me, but I only had eyes for Chris. As the avalanches sloughed off the slopes above and swished over our grotto, covering us completely, claustrophobia was intense. Meanwhile, I skipped over golden sands that lined a Tahitian lagoon, with my new-found wonders bouncing up and down, browned by the hot tropical sun. 'Waidaminit! I think we need more air!' Chris lurched forward to plunge his ice axe through the side of our icy tomb, creating a small window. The wind was still blowing furiously even though we were somewhat protected by 'the castle' above.

Forty-eight hours passed and a small break on the Nepalese side of the ridge appeared. We decided to make a run for it, descending the avalanche-prone slopes and groping our way through intermittent white-out conditions to the eventual safety of our one-person tent at Camp 3. Despite the bad conditions, the speed with which we descended astonished us, and a guarded optimism in our ability to get off the mountain without back-up support grew from the experience. The break in weather had been a short one. No sooner had the tent been located than it socked in again and the storm continued for yet another four days. We were reluctant to return to Base Camp as time was running close to the onset of the monsoon.

The storm passed. Calm and peace followed. We watched as tiny black dots spilled out of the tents of the Czech Camp 2 and made their way in a long file across the glacier. We sat back, ate a leisurely breakfast and took advantage of the hot sun to dry our boots, down gear and woollen clothes. One by one the Czechs started appearing. It was good to share stories and experiences, and before long a large crowd had gathered around our tent. I felt so sorry for the ones lagging behind. Here we all were, eating drinking, laughing and joking, while some poor bastard had as little as 180 m (600 ft) to go before he too could join in the fun. It might as well have been a hundred miles as he gasped for air with each breath seeming like his last, and loaded down with an enormous pack. It was like watching someone being slowly tortured; each one of us had endured a similar agony and understood so well. Finally everyone had arrived. The Czechs brought out several large cans of strawberries for the celebration. Having just witnessed the energy expended to arrive at this juicy morsel, the tastebuds exploded tenfold.

The same day we easily ascended 600 m (2,000 ft) to find the cave on the north ridge intact. Our ascent was facilitated by sharing the task of trail-breaking with the Czechs. Wishing each other well, we parted company at the base of the rock band. All we had to do was dig out the entrance to the cave and crawl in. What luxury.

The next day dawned brilliantly clear. We took turns to dress, as co-ordination of movements was essential in the cramped conditions. Chris went outside to attend to a call of nature. I decided to use an empty plastic bag from an old lunch sack. 'No sense in getting frostbite taking a dump,' I mumbled to myself. Glad that I had aimed well, I staggered outside to find Chris enthusiastically taking photos. The view was superb, but still the upper summit pyramid of Yalung Kang remained a mystery to us.

Without a cloud in the sky except a telltale plume off Everest, indicating strong winds higher up, we quickly re-ascended the slopes that led to the final rock step. A 6 m (20 ft) remnant of Scott's line was strung out on the rocks, rotting in the sun. Chris draped a sling and karabiner over a spike and took off, leading over the section. He soon disappeared over the lip. With a giant effort I finally heaved myself onto the scree-covered slopes above, gasping from the exertion, as a blast of wind hit. Gradually I recovered to look around. What a strange world, so alien and desolate. Like being on the moon. Chris said it reminded him of the south col of Everest when after four days, the tents they had erected had been reduced to ribbons by the fierce winds. Braced into the wind, we walked up a few hundred feet, our most urgent thought being to find shelter for the night.

Picking our way through the icy boulders and rocks we angled our way towards the lower part of the summit pyramid — called 'the croissant'. A thin surface of snow that lay over hard ice and small rocks was clearly a 'no vacancy' sign to our numbed brains and we moved on. To build a snow cave here would be impossible.

We would freeze in the effort of building it. My feet had frozen solid and I tottered along like a toy soldier with a wound-down battery. We decided to unrope. Dealing with the constant snagging of the rope on small rocks and outcrops of ice was consuming more energy than we cared to part with. The ground was easy and presented little danger from falling.

Chris dumped his pack and went scrambling over the slopes like a mountain goat. I sat down on a rock in a semi-stupor and waited, looking over glumly towards Yalung Kang. I wondered where that easy snow gully was we had hoped for? I put the thought aside. Maybe it will look more encouraging tomorrow, when we get closer. It was important to concentrate on more immediate matters. I was despondent about the condition of my feet, and concentrated all my efforts in pumping circulation through them. They were being very stubborn. After some time Chris returned. 'I think I've found a place, it's about another 30 minutes,' he reported breathlessly. After what seemed an eternity, we finally stopped. 'Here?' I asked him incredulously. 'It's the best I could find, it will have to do. I'm sorry,' he replied.

We set to digging out a narrow entrance on the lee of a rock no higher than 1 m (3 ft). Snow had drifted and collected on one side of it, and it was here that we burrowed and painstakingly formed a small hole. Several hours later we threaded our tired bodies into it, and kissed by the fading glow of twilight. Claustrophobia was acute. Every turn of the head sent a shower of ice crystals down our necks. I tried to control the shuddering by letting go and relaxing. The presence of death returned, sitting heavily on my shoulder, waiting. The stove sat balanced on our knees as we made brews late into the night. Morning came and slowly we coaxed our stiffened bodies into motion.

Out of the protective environment of the cave, the cold now settled deep into my bones. Slowly we walked towards the summit pyramid of Yalung Kang, eyes scanning, riveted for a moment on a route possibility, only to find it blocked, which meant retracing the same line moments later, coaxing, pleading. Each advance was met with steep rock and ice. Whichever way, we would be committed to several hundred feet of hard climbing. Just how difficult we could not say until we were actually there. We aimed for a large rock in the centre of the snowfield, took off our packs and sat down to discuss the matter further. I had an idea it was to be the end. With a sinking feeling we went over the situation as slowly and methodically as our oxygen-starved brains would allow.

May 19 was our 15th day on marginal supplies that we had stretched from our six-day food ration. We had one gas cartridge left. We could not really afford more than one more bivouac above 7,800 m (26,000 ft). This route almost guaranteed two and, with bad weather, the possibility of more before we were off the mountain. The weather was holding, but we did not even have an anchor to rappel off. The one we did have was needed to descend 'the castle'. It was a hard decision to turn back. Yet to succumb to the lure of our goal, the intense focus of the past few months, seemed to be leading us into a death trap. Two intense feelings were tearing me apart. Survival, life, told me to go down; another feeling told me to give the mountain everything I had and continue on. A distracting little devil popped into my head, 'We could easily climb the main summit from here. What do you think?' 'It's not worth it, Cherie. Bishnu and the Czech liaison officer are watching us through their binoculars, waiting for us to pull just such a stunt. We don't have a permit, remember?'

Choked with emotion, we hugged each other, took a last picture, forced down a bite to eat and descended at 8.30 in the morning to arrive at Camp 2 early that afternoon. The Czechs were there to greet us. 'You know I cried when I saw you two turn around,' one of them confided. 'Yeah!' Chris replied, 'I know, too bad the summit remained elusive, but I've got a feeling we'll be back.'

≈≈≈≈≈≈≈≈≈≈≈≈≈≈≈≈≈≈≈≈≈≈≈ *6* ≈≈≈≈≈≈≈≈≈≈≈≈≈≈≈≈≈≈≈≈≈≈≈

One climbs, one sees, one sees no longer but one has seen. There is an art of conducting oneself in the lower regions by the memory of what one saw higher up. When one can no longer see, one can at least know.

MOUNT ANALOGUE

RENE DAUMAL

≈≈

ALREADY THE spell had been broken by our encounter with the Czechs at Camp 2. In spite of all the kindness, warmth and comfort we received, that special feeling I cherished so much — of total oneness with Chris, the mountain and myself — was falling away. Silken veils dropping in layers, one by one, to the ground, trodden on and torn by rocks and climbing boots, finally to be left behind, discarded in remorse. With a fistful of codeine dispensed by the Czech doc, we now faced the long march back to Base Camp. My feet had been without sensation for four days, and Chris's too. Both of us were beginning to experience the painful process of thawing out. Invigorated by the oxygen-rich air and drawn by the anticipation of fresh food at Base Camp, we wandered along the moraine enclosed in our own private agony. By now I knew by heart every rock and stone, ice gully and rivulet. They were part of me, I was part of them.

Meanwhile, the entire Czech team had gathered at Camp 2 as two of their climbers made their way to the summit. The weather pattern was showing signs of a major change. The predominate westerlies were succumbing to a south-easterly pattern. After 20 May the monsoon was imminent; then the storms would increase in time and intensity, dropping hundreds of inches of snow on the surrounding slopes. Avalanche danger would be critical. The warmer temperature would melt the snow covering the crevasses, over which we now passed at best rather tenuously, transforming the passage into snarling, gaping jaws in every direction. Time was precious.

Spurred on by good weather, the two oldest Czech climbers had switched dramatically from what was to be a straightforward transport of supplies from Camp 4 to Camp 5, to a marathon push for the summit. Instead of depositing supplies and returning to the lower camp they continued on, carrying a minimum of food and a small cooking stove. In the excitement of leaving that morning, having decided to take advantage of the good weather, they had forgotten to include matches. This information had been relayed by two-way radio. All attention was riveted on two tiny dots inching their way towards the summit block. From our position we were unable to pick them out with the naked eye. The younger members, who had done the leading on the difficult rock band, were aware that the climbers had been without fluid for over 36 hours. They sat poised, ready to leap into action, either to rescue the climbers or to make their own summit bid. Suspense filled the air.

Gradually, the familiar green patch of Pang Pema grew larger in the distance. Between the jumble of rocks and boulders, a lone figure stood, large teapot in one hand and two cups in the other. It was Sanglai. Dancing gaily over the terrain, unaware of his incumbrances, he was greeting us in minutes. 'Oh Memsahib, your face', his voice filled with compassion as he stared at me. Had my nose fallen off, I wondered. I checked. No, it was still in place. Then my mind flashed to a similar scene when we came off Dhaulagiri. We had by chance bumped into Pasang Kami on the trail. He had said exactly the same words with the same expression. I hadn't a clue what he meant until I arrived in Pokhara and looked in a mirror. I barely recognised my face. Stress had left its telling mark. I supposed I looked like a real hag again, and resigned myself to the fact.

We sat down and Sanglai proceeded to help us off with our packs. We then methodically consumed the entire contents of the pot, cup after cup of steaming hot tea strongly fortified with milk and sugar. Slowly we moved back into action. Sanglai insisted, despite our protests, on carrying both packs plus the teapot, while we hobbled along behind to complete the last few yards to Base

Camp. We were met with smiles and hugs from Bishnu, the Czech liaison officer, and one or two sick members of the Czech team.

The most immediate thought on our minds was to examine our feet. We flopped down in the mess tent to submit to the exquisite luxury of Bishnu and Sanglai undoing our boots, untying laces, removing inner boots and layers of socks to reveal our naked feet. It was so nice to be taken care of that tears welled up in my eyes. Surprisingly, they didn't look too bad. Dusky big toes down to the metatarsal joints and varying degrees of colour changes on the other tips. Not much different to K2 or all the other times. From past experience it looked as though we would be losing toenails and some superficial layers of skin. I glumly wondered how much more abuse they could take before a major loss. We stuck them in tubs of warm water to complete the thawing process. Snuggled round the humming primus, we consumed further untold cups of tea and indulged in a fried egg — the greatest of all treats — along with some chapattis.

Sanglai had hinted on our way back at trouble brewing at Base Camp and now we were to extract, piece by piece, the full story. Apparently Sangay had been dealing with the Ghunsa people by selling our kerosene and food supplies. He had threatened to kill Sanglai with his ice axe, either on the walk out or on a dark street in Kathmandu, if he disclosed the truth. Bishnu had gone along with it initially but then had a change of heart. Sangay had threatened to report him to the police commissioner for supposed complicity if he supported Sanglai. Bishnu was in tears, begging forgiveness. Sanglai was shaking with fear. We were critically low on all food supplies — no wonder we could only get one egg each. We had been on low rations ourselves and were starving. Apparently no one expected we would be gone so long, even though we warned them of the possibility on leaving.

Sangay was in Ghunsa and expected to return at any time. It was a saving grace that our brains were pleasantly numbed by oxygen deprivation. We consulted with the Czech liaison officer who confirmed the situation was indeed as described by Bishnu and Sanglai. On going through Sangay's personal belongings we found a stash of pilfered items tucked away in a corner: Tang and chocolate bars, plus a climbing rope that had been missing since early in the trip.

All things we could have used on the mountain plus extra woollen hats, gloves and sunglasses, the radio and tape deck. On Sangay's return we called a meeting, with the Czech liaison officer present as an impartial witness, and went over the details and reasons for dismissal. We paid him sufficient rupees for his food and lodging to return to Kathmandu, which he refused to accept, and fired him. He was to be paid the balance in Kathmandu along with the rest of the staff.

Fortunately, we were distracted by the return of the Czech team supporting the two successful summiteers. What a fine example of human endurance and spirit. It was good to feel inspired and have our thoughts elevated to a different plane. Our young friends confided bitter disappointment not to have had a chance to make their own summit bid. The leader had called the expedition off in anticipation of the monsoon's arrival, and they felt severely thwarted, just as we had on the large expedition to K2 and now, for a different reason, on Yalung Kang.

On examination, the summiteers' frostbite appeared to be superficial. Nothing major would be lost, although as Chris put it, 'Like us, their corners have been rounded off a little.' Short-term memory loss, impaired verbal ability and abstract reasoning, along with labile emotions and depression, are the relatively short-lived effects of hypoxia. Medical research conducted by the 1981 Mount Everest Medical Expedition found after one year that these faculties had returned to normal. The only measurable change that remained below pre-hypoxia exposure was fine motor muscular skeletal function, measured by the speed of index-finger tapping. All participants in the experiment were found to have lower scores one year later.

Our porters and yaks arrived and we left shortly after. Refreshed after several days of inactivity without a pack, and descending to an even lower elevation, we felt as if we were walking on air. Charged with energy, and an enormous sense of relief, it was as if a giant weight had been removed and laughingly we took off and soared with the birds. The sweet perfume of soft earth and grass filled our nostrils. Inundated with the sounds, tastes and colours of a world we had left behind, like a yogi breaking a long fast, I almost suffered indigestion. I thought of the crowded streets of Kathmandu, then stepped further into the life of a metropolis, the cancer of western civilisation. What a privilege to have had such an experience, and what a debt to repay. Sanglai followed us, darting from boulder to boulder yapping at our heels like a stray dog.

We arrived in Ghunsa that afternoon, quickly cleared the police checkpoint, and arranged for porters to help carry our loads to an elevation of about 2,500 m (8,000 ft) where we would transfer to low altitude porters to complete the journey to Dharan. The four of us formed a tightly knit group, and we unanimously agreed to get the long journey over and done with as quickly as possible. However, there was a limit to how much walking Chris and I could endure each day. Our feet, swollen painfully with blisters from frostbite, were now experiencing a deep throbbing pressure, and red streaks followed the course of blood vessels. We took turns at giving each other shots of penicillin which took care of the infection.

Periodic heavy downpours were transforming the fields into iridescent green. The mountains lay heavy in cloud. Leeches were becoming a nuisance, trails were slippery with mud. At Serkatum we paid off the Bhotia and seemingly miraculously, out of the surrounding hills, filtered a handful of porters willing to complete the carry to Dharan. Sangay had been travelling several days ahead of us but it was here that he awaited us. We handed the situation over to our liaison officer. Bishnu explained that Sangay felt ashamed to travel back alone. Word of his dismissal had travelled magically in these remote areas. Although surprised by the request, it was hard to feel pity and we refused to let him travel with us.

The lurking dog now turned rabid and with foaming mouth and drooping tail, stalked our campsite. Climbing onto the rocks above, Sangay stood with a rock poised over Chris's head, threatening to smash it down on him. Chris stood below, motionless, not even a breath passed his lips. A critical moment passed. My respect for Bishnu grew as I watched him slowly diffuse Sangay's aggression. Night fell along with more rain. Sangay remained crouched beside a rock about 9 m (30 ft) away, refusing Bishnu's suggestions to

Leading up to the base of 'the castle'. On the scree slopes above we determine that the steep ice and rock of Yalung Kang's north face pose difficulties beyond our meagre resources. We turn around. (Photo Chris Chandler)

sleep in the small hamlet up the hill, or take shelter with the porters. We eyed him warily. The porters were singing around an open fire by an overhanging rock. Bishnu said they were warding off evil spirits that were lurking.

I noticed five plates of food prepared by Sanglai. Incredulously I asked, 'Is that for Sangay, you're doing that when he threatened to kill you and Chris?' Without turning or looking in my direction, Sanglai picked up the plate and replied, 'He is my brother,' and disappeared into the darkness. I lay awake most of the night experiencing the meaning of compassion. I think we all struggled with it and by morning a transformation had taken place. 'Sure,' Chris said. 'Feed him, let him follow us, save face, anything, I just want to avoid any further conflict.' The air had cleared and we felt lighter, but I had to admit we were fed up with the whole scene.

'Never again in the Himalayas. Why not take a trip to the Andes or Alaska? There's so much neat stuff out there, without the bullshit to deal with,' Chris ranted. 'Much cheaper, too. Yuk! All that deep snow and avalanche danger,' I raved. 'You're right, Cherie, it simply isn't worth it.' It was necessary to relieve some of the frustration we had experienced dealing with the negative aspects of the trip. It certainly hadn't evolved the way we had planned, our 'perfect little trip'.

A few days later we walked along the ridge, looking across at Makalu, Everest and Baruntse. 'Sure looks pretty, what would you say to picking out a nice classic line on Makalu,' I asked mischievously, just to see his reaction. Chris cast me a penetrating look. 'That might not be too bad, could even be fun.' Imperceptibly, a shift was taking place in our thinking. 'We certainly could

ABOVE: *The town of Ghunsa consists of about 25 dwellings, housing primarily Sherpas and Tibetans who fled from Tibet after the Chinese invasion to escape religious persecution. The Nepalese government generously opens its doors to these mountain people and allows them freedom to practise their Buddhist beliefs. The fresh mountain breeze flutters the prayer flags bestowing their blessings on those below.*

BELOW: *Drugs can be very helpful in specific individual emergencies (woman on right has an abscessed tooth), but the general health of the people is not so much determined by medical intervention as by their food, housing and culture. (Photo Chris Candler)*

apply some lessons learnt on this trip,' he added, 'which would be satisfying.' We took our last glimpse of Kanchenjunga through a grove of rhododendrons, sitting in a lush meadow, savouring the taste of wild strawberries and fresh yoghurt purchased from nearby herdsmen. 'I feel like we really know the mountain well — in some ways it would be nice to return,' Chris let the truth slip out. Without meaning to, I found myself confirming Chris's words.

In little more than a week Chris was standing in front of the desk at the Ministry of Tourism. 'Yes sir, we'd like to make reservations for Peak Kanchenjunga north face, along with north face Yalung Kang. As an alternative, our second choice would be Makalu.' We wanted to leave the choice of route open. The deed was done and we were soon winging our way back home.

Three years passed, filled with boat building, sailing and lesser climbs. We were granted permission to climb Kanchenjunga in 1982 but the trip had to be postponed due to a broken foot I received sailing, a scant month before our departure date. In the meantime we had also applied for permission to climb K2. We called it 'a second look at K2'. Suddenly everything seemed to be happening at once — no sooner had we sent off the peak fee for K2, summer of 1986, than we received word from the Nepalese government that they were granting permission for Kanchenjunga, but in winter and only six months before we were due in Pakistan for K2.

A turning point, a time of decision and deep introspection was taking place in our lives. Whether to continue in our careers, consolidating our positions and that strange concept, 'equity', or commit ourselves to honing the sharp edge of existence. Were we just hooked on the feeling of living on the edge or was it essential to our growth as human beings? Purity or profanity, maybe an everchanging mix? Doug Scott's question, 'Would I still climb if I were the last person on earth,' is an interesting one. I assume he is hinting that for most of us the answer would be no, since the mundane side of us would ask, 'Who would there be around to applaud, impress and astonish.' In my mind I tried to become the last person left after a holocaust and it is true that my priorities changed, but it wasn't for lack of an audience. Having inherited the collective consciousness of the world, simply to survive would seem an awesome enough task, but I wondered if, after a time, I wouldn't be tempted to play around on an outcrop of sunbaked granite, just for the fun of it.

We decided to dive in and accepted both climbs. We also planned the sailing trip to Valdez in Alaska beforehand, with the thought in mind of unlimited 'backyard' ice climbing to prepare for winter on Kanchenjunga. Two capsizes and unprecedented bad weather would send us limping into San Francisco, severely cutting short our desired destination. Instead of ice climbing, we spent the following year repairing the fairly extensive damage to the vessel. Chris tried to get a job in the area but we found there was a definite over-supply of doctors plus disinterest in one who lived anchored in the middle of the bay. 'Well, how can I get hold of you,' was the inevitable question. 'Just leave a message on my answering service and I'll call right back.'

That wasn't good enough. The problem was not absence of a telephone, but with communication on a different level, with acceptance of a lifestyle few people could understand. We took this as a fact of life, yet both of us were still sensitive to rejection and criticism and it hurt me to see this expressed in Chris.

When an offer was presented to resume his old job in Los Angeles, Chris gladly accepted. Even though it meant separation from each other for a week at a time and an arduous commute, we were both unwilling to return to L.A. to live full time. Slowly we were being sucked back into the rat race, and *Laylah* was a sanctuary, surrounded by water, wind and waves. Discovering the silhouette of a heron poised motionless on the bowsprit, listening to barking seals and squawking sea birds, were sights and sounds that nourished our tired spirits.

As part of an inner city Emergency Department in Los Angeles, Chris was faced nightly with the often coarse and uncensored ills of society. Brutal scenes stolen from a TV screen of stabbings and beatings were interspersed with runny noses and earaches, heart attacks, suicide attempts or the horrifying discovery of a toddler with oral or anal gonorrhea. The misery of man being served up on a large platter. Yet there were lighter moments, too, like the time Chris was confronted with a difficult extraction of a large pickle that refused to budge from a woman's vagina! The big question on everyone's mind was, 'Is it dill or kosher?' Just as Chris gave the mountains all his drive and energy, he also applied the same dedication to medicine, and it was good to hear him talk about his job with obvious satisfaction.

As the months rolled by and the departure date for our expedition grew closer, time became increasingly precious. Endless lists mounted for the procurement of equipment, food and medicine. With the increasing number of expeditions to the Himalayas, the chance of getting a manufacturer to donate clothing and equipment grants decreased — especially for such a small trip as ours with so little promise of success. At the same time, demands at work increased and pressure grew. The unhappy result was periodic outbursts of anger by Chris that left me at times afraid for my life. Teetering on the brink emotionally I hung on grimly, in the knowledge that Chris was as devastated as me at what was happening. We could never openly talk about the scenes, it was too threatening, so we continued as though they never happened. One day I asked, 'Do you want me to leave you?' 'There won't be anyone but you, sweetheart,' he answered, and I believed him. We were resolved to stick together to the end. During those tumultuous times I thought of seeking help through counselling or by talking to a close friend, but although no words were spoken, I knew Chris was pleading for confidentiality. To share the secret would be a betrayal of trust and so we bore the burden alone.

Meanwhile, Chris was offered the directorship of a small Emergency Room high in the Sierra Mountains. A perfect location for climbing and skiing, its altitude would provide plenty of opportunity for trauma management in a wilderness setting, plus the recognition and treatment of high altitude sickness, for which Chris was recognised as somewhat of an expert. The position fit him like a glove and we were both elated to be offered a respite from the city. We called Chris's folks in Seattle. 'I'm glad you two kids are finally coming to your senses,' his mother responded. Two expeditions six months apart, one being less than three months away, posed a sticky problem for hospital administrators, however. If we cancelled out on the trip Chris would have the job in the bag, and if we continued with our present plan they would keep the position open for his return. When Chris pushed for a written agreement the reply was, 'We don't want to sign a contract with a dead man.' We both retracted at the response and later Chris said, 'It's hard for a non-climber to understand.'

It was midnight as we lay soaking in steaming hot springs located on the outside of town. The mountains glowed in the light of a full moon. It seemed we were being given another chance to reconsider our priorities and we took the opportunity seriously. There really wasn't any desperate reason to continue our trip as planned, and the job appeared seductively attractive. But as Chris said, 'This job and others like it, will always be there.'

We were both eager for a hard climb and realised this one would probably be the hardest climb of our lives. We were resolved on the absolute necessity for a Base Camp manager to prevent a recurrence of the problems we had experienced in 1981. We needed an amicable but firm presence — to prevent a premature desertion should we be late returning; to oversee operations; to manage supplies, etc. This time we couldn't afford any last minute changes — dependability was essential. Yet how does one go about asking someone to leave their job in order to walk over 160 km (100 miles), then sit around for four to six weeks at 5,200 m (17,000 ft), in the dead of winter, with a group of potential thieves, possibly suffering from dysentry, while waiting to see if we would come off the mountain or not? Chris thought that to ask another climber would be inviting trouble. Boredom may lead he or she on some solitary exploration of surrounding peaks with the possibility of landing in big trouble. We didn't want to have to worry about such eventualities. My roving eye landed on a potential candidate. A fellow co-worker in the intensive care unit where I worked, Lori Orlando, was planning an extended holiday to Europe. It was to be her first visit overseas.

Lori had a bubbling, vivacious personality and could handle the most difficult characters, from cleaning lady to chief of surgery, with an easy skill and charm. It was an invaluable asset, and her naturally optimistic outlook would help boost staff morale during the long and difficult sojourn. Gradually, as I got to know her more, I discovered she had never done any climbing or even much hiking before, but liked to swim and cycle. In fact she had swum the English Channel. With that kind of drive I knew she was capable of the endurance required, and I ran home to report my find enthusiastically to Chris. 'Well, why don't you ask her over and we'll put it to her.' He too, was interested.

Her large black eyes stared at us in disbelief as I lay out our plans and her potential role. 'Let me think about it.' It was a fair reply. With the help of slide shows and a great deal of reading, Lori became somewhat of an armchair mountaineer. In addition, we overwhelmed her with suitably embellished, first-hand accounts of all the horrors she would be likely to face: poverty, filth, sickness and lack of medical facilities, not to mention the absence of hot showers and a soft mattress for three months. 'You may not have a good time, but I can guarantee you will be a changed person from the experience,' I joked with her, hoping not to sound too negative.

I know we had appealed to Lori's sense of adventure and were winning her over fair and square, despite her family's grave misgivings. Self-interest was countered by a strong sense of responsibility for another human being, and it was important to be as honest as possible about what she was getting into, including the possibility of our deaths and her role should that happen. 'You said at 17,000 feet it's impossible to gain weight,' she asked unbelievingly. 'Sure, you'll lose weight without even trying. But you'll gain it again as soon as you reach sea level and start eating normally,' I added. But she wasn't listening, 'Sure I'll go.' She had made up her mind at last. We sighed in relief. Base Camp manager was checked off the list as the world's highest fat-farm lay waiting.

Things were beginning to take shape. Various food and equipment people were offering free or cost price equipment. I began making overboots styled on the advice of the Burgess twins, Adrian and Allen, who had several experiences of Himalayan climbing in winter, including being 'blown off' Everest. With one-piece, Gortex-covered, down suits and their own self-made overboots which fitted snugly over their plastic double boots, they claimed their feet were WARM. Memories of my own experience with Terry on our ascent of Gangchimpo in the Jugal Himal in mid-December were still vivid. As a south-face route, we were fortunate to have the sun for four to five hours a day before it dipped behind a distant ridge. As soon as it disappeared our bodies stiffened with cold and our feet became wooden. The inconvenience of constantly having to stop to warm up feet on each other's stomachs usually caused us to set up camp early in the afternoon.

That time we were wearing traditional leather double boots and standard overboots. Chris and I were impressed by the advice of the twins and decided that we too would have WARM feet. The finished overboots looked promising. The chances of more serious loss of tissue increases after each freezing episode, and moreover it takes less and less time to succumb. We had been exposed to cold a sufficient number of times over the years to realise we must exercise extreme care.

My mother, on a precious visit from Australia, quickly got sucked into the excitement of trip preparations by sewing up sets of lightweight Gortex jackets and pants of special design by Louise Sumner. Clothing that was lightweight, yet durable and easily condensed, simply was not available commercially. Lori and I became involved in putting together a fairly comprehensive medical kit that would serve not only the staff and our own personal needs, but those of the local population as well. This was part of the trip that we all anticipated as being fun: meeting the Nepalese people on a more meaningful and intimate level than any average tourist could hope for. We also saw it as an opportunity to repay a small part of the debt we owed: the privilege of being born into a technically advanced, wealthy society, and reaping the benefits thereof.

I was collecting the most recent articles and studies of high altitude sickness and pulmonary and cerebral oedema, to review with Chris. There is a group of now well recognised and defined signs and symptoms that occur as a result of the body's maladaptation to lowered oxygen concentration. These include headache, lassitude, shortness of breath and weakness, plus a multitude of other subtle changes. They all occur primarily as a result of abnormal fluid shifts on a cellular level, eventually causing the brain and lungs to become boggy and waterlogged. Death quickly ensues. 'Take a look at this book, *Mountain Sickness — Prevention, Recognition and Treatment* by Peter Hackett MD,' Chris said, 'it's really excellent. Make sure Lori has a copy and reads it cover to cover and we'll keep this one ourselves.'

'Yeah, here's an interesting article by Brownie Schoene MD from his studies on Mount McKinley, I replied. He says ... "Cold environment is almost as universal a factor as hypoxia in the development of high altitude pulmonary oedema — but more studies

need to be done before it can be said it's a predisposing factor."
Huh! I suppose we should be extra cautious due to winter conditions. He finishes off the article with, "The identity of the event or
the mediator which initiates the leak still remains a mystery."'

'Well, regardless,' Chris added, 'the rules still remain the same —
preventing problems by a slow and measured rate of ascent, and
descending as quickly as possible at the first signs of trouble. But
we should keep in mind, due to the lower barometric pressure in
winter, that it's going to be more difficult than in summer for us to
acclimatise to the same altitude.' It was understood that we each
took the responsibility of being 'watchdogs' for one another. Subtle
behavioural changes such as irritability, irrational behaviour and
lassitude are difficult symptoms to recognise if you are the affected
individual whose judgement, by the very nature of the situation, is
impaired.

After a long night's work, Lori and I would invariably meet to
talk over her concerns. 'You and Chris have got to take two-way
radios, its an absolute must. How else will I know if anything is
wrong?' Lori insisted emphatically. 'Look, Lori, the reason we
don't take radios is that they're expensive, often have a large import
tax levied, are heavy to carry and sometimes don't work in the
cold. Just imagine if you and the staff all gave up and left Base
Camp for Kathmandu, when the only thing dead was the batteries.
We are really going to be wasted when we come off and are going
to need you there waiting. Besides,' I said matter of factly, 'above
20,000 feet you'll be able to watch our progress with binoculars,
and even if something did go wrong, there's not much you're
going to be able to do about it, whether you're in radio contact or
watching us with binoculars.' The matter was closed. Deep inside
was another reason why Chris and I preferred lack of communication with Base Camp. The radio was a symbolic link to the outside
world, the umbilical cord we chose to sever.

It had been a particularly busy night. We were just about to
knock off work when Lori came up to me. 'Cherie, I need to talk to
you.'

'Go right ahead.'

'No, I mean, where we won't be disturbed.'

'I'll meet you in the vestibule, by the elevators.' I groaned internally. All I wanted to do was bike home and drop into a deadening sleep.

She was waiting there. 'I had a dream I have to tell you about.' She clutched my arm, and with a faraway look on her face, stared off into the distant void. 'There are two, no that's not right, three people and I can see you're very close to the top.' Wrong! I was amused, Chris and I would be climbing alone. 'It's not clear to me if you've reached the summit or if you're coming back down. Two people are climbing together, the other person is sitting by himself, underneath some rocks, as though he's watching and guiding the other two.' Maybe some Freudian thing like the alter ego, I wondered, beginning to get interested. 'There's some kind of problem with communication, almost like a language barrier between the two people. One person is yelling at the other — something's terribly wrong, but I can't work it out,' she screwed up her face in concentration.

I started to freeze up inside. She was really stepping on a sensitive spot now. I didn't want to hear any more. I knew Chris and I had our problems but they always dissolved magically when we were in a difficult situation. We weren't the stereotyped, bickering married couple. I knew that lovers and couples emotionally involved weren't supposed to climb together for fear that personal feelings would override good judgment. Chris and I just laughed at these 'rules' made by people who have no idea of the joy of completeness one can feel. Besides, anyone who has been on an expedition can tell you, if they are honest, that keeping lovers apart is no guarantee of harmony and good judgement — far from it, feelings of hostility can run very deep among all the climbers.

Lori went on. 'One of the climbers looks like he doesn't know what he's doing, like he's not used to climbing.' With this I nearly exploded inside. I couldn't believe what I was hearing. What did she think she was doing, anyway, playing these head trips on me? I walked over to the lift and pressed the button. 'There will be much falling,' her voice echoed, trailing after me.

'So, do we live or do we die?' I asked rather sardonically.

'That won't be known until the very last moment.' The elevator had arrived and I was about to step inside. 'Wait, there's something else I forgot to tell you. It's about gloves, you lose or drop one, yes,' she was vague and wandering in thought. She turned to me directly and blurted out, 'Cherie, you've got to do something about your hands, promise me.'

I was holding the door open. 'Don't worry about it, Lori, we always take along a whole wardrobe of gloves for extras. Hands are right under our noses so we can see if there's a problem and can quickly warm them up in armpits or on a stomach, even pee on them if we have to. It's the feet you should feel concerned about. I'm off now — see you Friday.' I let the door close between us.

It was good to be outside and feel the fresh air on my face. I pumped vigorously up the steep hills of San Francisco to reach a crest and plummet down again. The rush of wind caused the tears streaming from my eyes to be flattened against reddened cheeks. I was angry, I just didn't need to hear stuff like that. I'd had enough problems dealing with my own dreams. One that was particularly vivid was of being overcome by a large snow avalanche just below 'the castle' on the north ridge. As the snow enveloped me I made some futile efforts at swimming. I soon realised I was dead. Floating around in a black void I reached out to touch familiar objects around the bed, only to have my hand pass through them — I was filled with terror as I looked down and saw Chris and myself lying beside each other embraced in death. I finally woke up to realise I wasn't ready to die yet. Well, we won't even be on that route anyway, I comforted myself later. I wanted to talk things over with Chris, hinting at cancelling the expedition. Unwisely, I chose the wrong time, when he was exhausted after returning from Los Angeles. He flew off the deep end, and I never brought it up again.

By now I had reached the dinghy dock and started rowing out to the boat. Chris was waiting, 'How was work?' 'Fine. Lori's been doing a few head trips on me. If she keeps it up she can forget about even coming.' I didn't see her for a while. When I did, she seemed her usual happy, cheerful self, making no mention of her dream. We never spoke of it again and I soon forgot it. Apparently she had seen a few psychics to talk over her plans for the future and as she put it, 'To find out if we would reach the summit or not.' Separately, the psychics had agreed 'that everything was going to turn out OK', but they were unwilling to predict a summit success or failure. One told her she could see a little devil popping around

Lori's shoulders and head and she should dispel it as it would only bring harm. I wondered if the psychic was alluding to the fascination Lori had for Chris, but kept my insecure thoughts to myself. After all, Chris had every opportunity to mess around with other women if he wanted to, why should he choose now? Maybe this was time for me to face the same hurt Terry had experienced on K2. There wasn't any way to fight it. What happens happens and I had to face the future with equanimity.

As if enough things weren't happening, I tore a muscle in my shoulder which gave me a painful upper back and neck requiring anti-inflammatory and muscle relaxant drugs, and my knee began 'locking' at more and more frequent intervals, the result of an old climbing injury. I was an orthopaedic wreck. An excellent sports doctor took a quick look inside to find not only the major ligaments in my left knee withered up or 'gone', but the meniscus had a large tear which was causing the troublesome locking. He removed the offending part. I was up walking the same day and running with a splint at the end of the week. A good thing too, as our departure date was three weeks away.

Things were coming together in a climactic series of last minute deadlines. It was the night before Lori's and my flight to Seattle. Chris was following in the van loaded up with all the expedition gear which we planned to pile on the Thai flight to Bangkok and Kathmandu as unaccompanied luggage. I was involved in last minute sewing and packing. Chris had been held up in peak hour traffic for two and a half hours instead of the usual 30 minutes. He came in looking drained. I was in the process of writing a note to tape on the dryer in the coin-operated laundromat. It said: 'Please do not remove clothes from dryer before drying complete. Time important — early morning plane to catch. Thanks, Cherie.' When I explained to Chris that I'd been trying to dry a down jacket all afternoon that I wanted to throw in as an extra, but some jerk kept removing it, he tuned in to my irritation immediately and grabbed the note saying, 'Let me take care of it.'

I had a sinking feeling it was the wrong thing to do but before I knew it, he was out of the door and gone. After a while the sound of yelling came filtering into my consciousness. I recognised one of the voices to be Chris's. Ten minutes passed. No sign of Chris. I went down to see what was going on and found the flashing lights of a patrol car. An argument had broken out in the laundry with someone like the deputy sheriff's wife and her son, who had removed the jacket from the dryer. Taking offence at Chris, he had come from behind with a choke-hold. Chris had bitten the youth's arm in order to release his hold and then chased him down the road. I watched helplessly as the handcuffs snapped around Chris's wrists. He had broken out in a cold clammy sweat, and his shirt was soaked through. I went up and hugged him, 'Don't worry sweetheart, it's going to be OK.'

The incident totally devastated both of us. Like a glaring spotlight that blotted out all peripheral vision, the arrest focused on the problem of Chris's anger. Something that until now had just been between the two of us lay open and exposed. Neither of us wanted to face what we saw. Barely able to find the correct change and dial, I called Gary — a good friend who had been helping us out with the packing. I managed to choke out a few appropriate words, 'Would you help me bail out Chris?' He answered, 'The more I have to do with this trip and you two, the more it's like watching something from *Raiders of the Lost Ark*.' I managed a smile.

Because of the unexpected hold-up, Lori and I missed the plane. No matter — far better to be setting off together as a unit instead of being separated. We stuffed ourselves in among the piles of duffles and packs, giggling in relief over the smallest things. All our wordly possessions had been sold to meet the financial burden of the trip. Ahead lay the untrodden future. The past was behind us. For all the grief, tears would not wash away one part of it.

7

*T*o think God will protect you and your
children is erroneous.
He has already given us everything to cause the
end of suffering.

STEPHEN LEVINE

OUR EARS popped and seat belts snapped closed as the plane descended to make its final drop into Kathmandu. We craned our necks out of the window, impatient for our first glimpse of the valley and the surrounding peaks, clad heavily in cloud. 'Oooh! it's so pretty,' drooled Lori. 'Look at the hillsides carved so meticulously by the terraces.' Excitement welled up inside me and I squeezed Chris's hand. It felt like we were coming home. 'Looks dry,' Chris commented. 'It doesn't seem like the snow level is down too far. What do you reckon Cherie, 13,000 to 14,000 feet?' 'Yeah! A light dusting about the tree line or maybe a bit higher,' I replied, 'despite the heavy cloud cover.'

One of our major concerns was being able to get the expedition supplies up to Base Camp level. My previous experience mid-December in the Jugal Himal had given us several feet of snow as low as 3,600 m (12,000 ft). Encountering conditions like that would be sounding the death knoll to the success of our trip. Even a large cash bonus used as an incentive to lure either yak or man from sheltered stable or hearth would be a task in itself, when there was no guarantee of success. We were prepared to triple the normal wage, and knew beyond that it was out of our hands. November weather is normally sunny and dry.

The Nepalese government does not object to expeditions occupying Base Camp and establishing Camp 1, providing they don't occupy it. All of us were attracted by the idea of arriving early in order to acclimatise fully in the good weather and then, on 1 December, to climb the mountain as quickly as possibly before the heavy winter storms hit after Christmas. However, Mike Cheney of Sherpa Co-operative had warned us of the Diwali Festival from 24–27 November which is observed as a national holiday for Hindus and Tihar. To arrive amidst these celebrations would be frustrating as government offices would be closed. After all, November was a period of 'rest' for the mountains also.

With our own set of hold-ups in San Francisco we did not leave Seattle until 5 November. We were well aware that many so-called winter expeditions had been on the mountain since the beginning of November, putting in the route but not officially 'occupying' camps until 1 December to comply with the rules. Keenly aware of our disadvantage, we consoled ourselves that this would at least be a 'true' winter expedition. The fact that the Poles had climbed Makalu as late as 12 January and that Everest had now been climbed as many as three times in winter, helped allay our nervousness at having missed this tactical advantage, through circumstances beyond our control.

A representative from Sherpa Co-operative was anxiously await-ing our arrival. He finally spotted us in the crowd and in a mixture of exasperation and relief welcomed us. 'We've been coming to the airport every day for a week. Where have you been?' We muttered our apologies over piles of lists and forms. We passed through customs quickly, shuffled along by officials with Steve Jorgenson's winter trip to Pumori. 'What do you think Cherie, shall we do it to Lori?' Chris turned to me as we all piled into the cab. Why not? 'The Himalayan View, thank you,' Chris gave instructions to the eager driver, who pulled out into the throng of people, seemingly unaware of the trail of victims possibly strewn behind us. For passage through the streets of Kathmandu, the horn is omnipotent.

Lori's mouth was agape. It doubled our enjoyment just to watch her reactions. 'A police officer back there wanted me to buy him some duty free liquor.' 'You didn't did you?' we both asked, aghast. 'No, but only because 20 different other people wanted me either to change money, take a taxi to their hotel, or buy some hashish.' 'Welcome to Kathmandu!' we all laughed.

Despite our efforts at trying to avoid the festivals, we had arrived in the middle of one anyway. We welcomed the opportunity to relax and become sane individuals again after the hectic months of preparation. Lori was uniformly unimpressed by Kathmandu. I was disappointed she did not share our enthusiasm and winced at her complaints — couldn't she just hold her breath as diesel fumes belched forth from passing vehicles? 'It's just culture shock Lori, after a while you'll find yourself side-stepping the crap without even noticing it. You'll be able to see Kathmandu for the jewel it really is.'

'We can control safe landing of spacecraft on the moon, but can't control the poison from our engines,' Lori observed. The pollution of the valley did seem particularly bad. Stagnant air was trapped by the surrounding foothills and there were frequent morning fogs. In a country that was struggling just to meet high fuel costs and maintain its vehicles, how could it possibly consider costly conversion to anti-pollution devices? Greater use of shuttle buses and innovative electrical and gas engines would help, but the real culprits seemed to be the buses and trucks that thundered constantly to and from India and outlying towns. Heavy pollution over the years was causing an accelerated rate of decay to the medieval structure that made Kathmandu a living museum. Since the introduction of the automobile, what had stood for centuries was beginning to crumble and decay in a matter of years. Renovation efforts couldn't keep abreast of the destruction, not to mention the health hazard imposed on the population.

As dawn was breaking, we chose a fragrant lei of blossoms from a street vendor and visited a favourite temple. We watched as Ganesh and Langtang Himal became bathed in alpen glow. Then the streets were quiet, the peace broken only by the sound of a ringing bell or crying child. Incense took the place of diesel fumes.

On another night we ventured forth along the narrow cobbled streets of the bazaar, lit only by the flickering glow of butter lamps, to discover a group of Newari singers and musicians who had gathered around a temple to pass the chillum, chant the ancient scriptures and revel in the rhythm of their music. On the one hand Kathmandu was reeling under the impact of the outside world, but these sights and sounds remained inviolate.

The festival was over and we could now begin business. A major blow to us was learning that Sanglai would not be accompanying us as sardar. It was hard to disguise our shock and disappointment

— hadn't we counted on him and thought so fondly of him over the years as being an integral part of our trip? Cheney brushed it aside lightly. 'It was Sanglai's choice, he was going off with some trekkers as sardar — they wanted him also. He's sending his brother as a replacement, who has also worked for and was very well liked by Doug Scott, who runs the same low budget operations as you two. I'll send Mongol over to the Himalayan View for you to meet, with the cook Tirthay who is his best friend. They are a very close bunch, they share quarters with one another in Kathmandu and work very well together.'

Chris was angry and I was too, but it was Sanglai's choice. The least Cheney could have done was to write to us and let us know ahead of time. Next time we would make our own arrangements privately instead of going through an agency. It was unfortunate news; when you are out on a limb on a big mountain like Kanchenjunga, it's nice to know you can rely on someone.

We all sat rather stiffly in a circle around a table that was too small for anything but a grimy pot of tea and cups so thick you could play ball with them. One of the legs of the table was shorter than the others, causing the table to lurch dangerously back and forth. The usual crowd of curious onlookers stood by watching. We were in the courtyard of the Himalayan View, and Chris and I were giving the three candidates jaded looks. 'Well, what are your qualifications?' Chris was curt and to the point. Mongol was quiet and shy like his brother, but displayed enough underlying assertiveness to show us he really wanted the job, along with his chosen crew of helpers: Tirthay as cook and Mingma as mail-runner and kitchen boy. It was difficult at first to work out Mongol's level of English comprehension. Since he was so eager to please, he said yes to almost everything. Yes, he did know how to climb and had taken a course for climbing Sherpas; he knew how to climb out of a crevasse and set up a belay. Yes, he had accompanied Doug Scott on some of his trips, along with Sanglai, and had climbed to 6,000 m (20,000 ft), and yes, this was his first time as sardar.

Unfortunately, it was only the last statement that we knew for a fact was probably true. Chris continued to drill Mongol on the various aspects of how he expected the trip to be run to prevent any recurrences of the problems we had encountered in 1981. All bags would be locked and numbered, with precise lists of contents recorded in a book. The loads would be checked systematically at periods throughout the trip. Mongol would be accountable for missing supplies or equipment either to Lori as Base Camp manager, or directly to Chris. This carefully rehearsed, hard-nosed approach was contrary to our natures but we both felt it necessary.

Mongol absorbed Chris's instructions in deadly earnest. We both felt relieved that we had started out on the right foot. The inspection of equipment was done smoothly and quickly and all three seemed happy and pleased with their issue. It was hard not to make constant comparisons with Kusang and Sangay, but already a mood of optimism was growing. 'Well, Mongol seems quite willing to go along with anything we say, I think we'll have a good crew,' Chris confided to Lori and me after we bade them farewell. 'Nonetheless, when we split up tomorrow for our various shopping trips, check everything, write it down and keep receipts. Mongol and I will be going to the ministry with Cheney for a briefing, so it will be in your hands.'

In a matter of three days most of the shopping for food and cooking utensils had been done, except for a few last-minute things. The bureaucratic side of the expedition was not going so smoothly. We still had no liaison officer and we resolved to depart without one, leaving it up to the government to get their act together. We could wait no longer. But there was still more bad news. Less than two months before our departure from the States, we had received a letter from Cheney informing us that the government had increased fees for 7,800 m (26,000 ft) peaks from $1,000 to $2,400. Our original application asked for Kanchenjunga main peak as well as Yalung Kang, with a $500 deposit on each. We wanted to have the choice of having a good try on Yalung Kang but if it proved too difficult, still be able to make a go for Kanchenjunga without being stymied by red tape. With the heavy increase in fees, we had cancelled out on Yalung Kang and asked Cheney to transfer the deposit over to the main peak. He had sent a quick note in reply — 'no problem'. Now Mr Shrestha at the ministry, unmoved by any sense of fairness, was saying it couldn't be done!

Cheney, Chris and I stood outside Mr Shrestha's office waiting for the final briefing. 'I wonder if we explained to him we only

have so much money in the budget ...' I began. Cheney interrupted, 'Oh come on now, a doctor crying poor? Do you think he's
going to buy that one? There's always more money!' His tone had
traces of sarcasm. Cheney hit a trigger point and I snapped back.
'For one thing, would you mind letting me finish. You're right,
there is always more money, but not out of our pockets. That
money was earmarked for a mini aid project we had wanted to
invest in for the people of Ghunsa! This cancels out any extra
spending money we might have for such a thing.'

Chris had an ongoing correspondence with B.A. Coburn, the
Unesco adviser who encouraged us with the idea of installing
auxiliary back boiler water heaters in several of the larger homes in
Ghunsa for the purpose of saving on firewood used in cooking and
heating water. These simple, low cost but remarkably effective
devices installed in the back or side of the traditional fire pit, have
tremendous potential for firewood-saving, other than perhaps
hydro-electricity. With the likelihood of restrictions crossing the
Tibetan-Nepalese border loosening up and the availability of easily
accessible passes in the Kanchenjunga region, we felt it would only
be a matter of time before the invasion of trekkers and climbers to
the area would begin causing serious deforestation problems, similar to those in the Everest region. We had even thought of spread-
ing the idea among other climbers so that in a matter of a few
years, every house could be fitted with one if a contribution was
made by each expedition to the area.

Rather than return home feeling unfulfilled if conditions on the
mountains were too severe for climbing, another idea was to spend
time in Ghunsa testing people's reactions and their willingness to
adopt a more scientific approach to the management of composting
human waste. At present it was simply mixed with straw, leaves
and yak dung and spread on the fields, contributing greatly to the
spread of gastro-intestinal diseases. If we could stimulate some
interest and support, we planned to return in warmer months —
accompanied by our children as an educational experience for them
— to implement the project.

Not only did we have to absorb the sudden and expected rise in
peak fees, the overall rise in the cost of porters from 26 to 40 rupees
a day and the uncertain cost of transport above Ghunsa, but now

the refusal to transfer the deposit. As Cheney had predicted, Mr Shrestha was unmoved. Chris put his arm around me as we walked out of the office, 'Let's get out of here and go climbing!' 'Sounds like a great idea, I replied.' We were frustrated and looked towards our mountain for solace.

One improvement for travellers in recent years had been the introduction of the 'night coach', a bus that runs express to Dharan in a slick and comfortable 12 hours, eliminating the 18-hour bone-shaking special. They were all fitted with reclining seats and head-rests and the only thing that rode on the roof was luggage. Lori and I managed, with the help of the people at the Himalayan View and the drivers themselves, to get our gear loaded from the hotel room into six rickshaws stacked 2.5 m (8 ft) high with duffles and packs. We jogged alongside, Lori at the head of the procession and me following along at the tail in an effort to keep everyone together in the congested streets. Tourists clicked their cameras, children ran alongside, old men smiled and sari-clad women stared in disbelief at the spectacle. The policeman's whistle dropped out of his mouth but it didn't matter, the traffic had stopped anyway.

The responsibility of being in charge of the operation shielded me from feeling exposed to so many staring eyes, until it was disco-vered we had arrived at the wrong bus terminal! Now, giggling in embarrassment, with Lori squealing in front that she had a stitch and needed to 'pee', we herded our flock back to the streets and on another mile to the correct departure point. Chris had been held up with last minute details and was to meet us there. We waited, but there was no sign of him. We quickly unloaded and got everything on top of the bus and firmly secured. Then Tirthay remembered he had left his boots behind — in the house where he lived on the other side of Kathmandu. We loaded him into a taxi which took off at an impressive speed and then got caught in a traffic jam less than 45 m (150 ft) from the bus station.

It was 4.30 pm, the bus was due to leave at 5 pm precisely. Still no sign of Chris. At 4.45 pm, Chris appeared with a police officer at his side. Trouble, I wondered? 'Cherie, Lori, I'd like you to meet inspector Bharat Chudal, the liaison officer who will be accom-panying us.' 'Pleased to meet you,' he bowed politely. He had to raise his voice as the bus had started to warm up its engines. 'I have to hurry home and tell my wife, she does not know yet of my plans, and I have to change my clothes.' 'Isn't that kind of short notice for a three-month expedition?' I ventured. 'Yes but she will be happy for me, I only found out myself 20 minutes ago.' He disappeared into the crowd. Chris shrugged his shoulders, 'He said he lives just around the corner.' 'At least we're consistent,' Lori laughed and we joined in.

It was time for the passengers to board. Chris checked with the driver, who confirmed that there would be no waiting for latecomers. The first of the two Dharan buses pulled out. I was beginning to feel a little desperate until I saw Bharat with a beaming face, and behind him Tirthay looking troubled. He hadn't been able to pick up his boots. Too bad.

The journey was comfortable for all of us except Lori, who had not come to terms with the problem of how she was going to relieve herself. 'I just won't drink,' she said stubbornly. 'That's only going to last so long, three days at best,' Chris gently chided her.

The walk so far from Hille had been enjoyable. We set up camp on the ridge at about 2,700 m (9,000 ft). It was sunset and the peaks were bathed in soft pinks and golds slowly fading into a frigid blue. The grass crunched under out footsteps. Tomorrow we would be descending the ridge into Dobhan. My freshly-operated knee seemed to be working and the pain in my neck and back was held in check by anti-inflammatory drugs. Carrying a pack didn't seem to make it worse. I wanted to get off the medication as soon as possible and had tried several times which resulted in a crippling flare-up of the symptoms. One of the side effects of the drug Feldene is a 'cortisone-like' effect of water retention, hardly something I wanted to encourage at high altitude for fear of increasing the risk of cerebral and pulmonary oedema. Another result of prolonged use of the drug is possible bone marrow depression which could make the user more susceptible to infections.

We were all suffering from colds and runny noses, but mine had gone to my chest causing painful breathing and coughing, and a feeling of being short of breath. Chris wasn't sure whether it was the altitude, bronchitis, early pneumonia or a combination of all three. My chest certainly felt quite gurgling and wet. In addition, I was developing sharp, knife-life stabbing pains in my groin and abdomen when I walked. Was I developing a pelvic infection too? How much of all this could be attributed to the Feldene? Chris decided to treat everything with a lengthy course of Septra D.S. and advised me to stop taking the Feldene.

The 1,800 m (6,000 ft) descent into the valley conviced me to put the splint on my knee, and I kept it on after several painful displacements of the joint. It registered its complaint by a large swelling. The splint worked like a dream but its effect on the porters, with their concerned looks and overprotective gestures, was making me feel like a cripple! Chris and I were both worried about the general shape I was in. We discussed the possibility of Chris soloing if things didn't improve, with me as back-up support lower on the mountain. They were sobering thoughts but we remained overall guardedly optimistic. After all, hadn't Pete Boardman badly injured his ankle on the approach to Kanchenjunga, so severely that it was necessary for him to be carried in a straw basket almost to Base Camp? He still managed to reach the summit. I changed from Feldene to Clinoril, a drug similar in its mode of action, with the hope of lessening the side effects, and I resolved to start tapering the dosage. I also lightened the load I was carrying by about 10 kg (20 lb).

Bharat had been born in his family's house, about 300 m (1,000 ft) above the junction of the Tamur River and the Maiwa Khola. He invited us to share a meal and meet his family, and we anticipated the special occasion with pleasure. Bharat ran ahead to warn the household of our intended visit. He then met us on the trail to escort us to his house. The farmers working in the nearby fields or carrying loads on the trail greeted Bharat in a way that made it obvious to us he was both well liked and held in a position of extreme respect. The workers would kneel or bow before him, he would touch them lightly on the head or shoulder and say a few benevolent words. Bharat was a high caste Brahmin who wore the sacred thread, was a sensitive and intelligent man and as such enjoyed literature, the beauty of nature, and wrote poetry for relaxation.

His family's house or, more precisely, group of mud brick dwellings with thatched roofs and carved wooden windows, was situated around a central courtyard where the women sifted grain and children played. Orange and apricot orchards caught my eye and further on there were lush plots of vegetables. One of Bharat's brothers was a horticulturist, and scientific instruments and measuring devices were scattered in the fields. In the distance, framed by scarlet poinsettias, lay Kumbhakarna, 'the sleeping giant'. Known to westerners as Jannu, it forms part of the Kanchenjunga massif.

We were introduced to all the male members of the family. Lori and I made a point of smiling and acknowledging the women, whose existence would have been otherwise ignored. Despite the traditional appearance of the household we learnt that Bharat's father had married a woman of a lower caste, and Bharat himself had divorced his first Brahmin wife to take a lower caste woman as his second wife. The inconsistencies were puzzling, for Bharat's mother was not allowed to cook the rice and dahl which are considered ritual foods. The meal was prepared by his full caste Brahmin sister-in-law. We were invited to wash by fresh spring water that bubbled from a stone pipe. The bathing area was paved with slate and kept spotlessly clean. It also provided welcome privacy.

At the beginning of each meal it was necessary to wash not only hands but also feet, so that nothing unclean would be brought to the eating area. Taking advantage of the situation, Lori and I took a full bath. Bharat explained that the hearth where the rice was cooked must be kept extremely pure. No one of a lower caste or temporarily impure such as a menstruating woman may enter. Cow dung mixed with mud paste had been spread over the entire cooking area in preparation for the meal. We were beginning to realise that eating lunch was not to be a liesurely social event — we were capable of polluting others and thus causing them to lose their caste! No wonder Bharat was coaching us so carefully to stay precisely in our own eating area and be careful not to touch a common eating vessel.

Our hostess had removed her blouse which was not apparently entirely pure, and wrapped a cotton sari around her breasts. She did not eat or even taste the food until everyone else had been served, for in doing so she would pollute it by the contact with her saliva, and then if she touched the food again it would all become polluted.

She stayed a safe distance off, dropping the second helpings of dahl and yoghurt onto our plates. The whole experience was interesting but more than a little disconcerting, for what was a simple act of dining etiquette to the Hindu was an elaborate ritual to us. As instructed by Bharat, we carefully went outside without touching anything or anyone and washed our hands and feet again.

Before leaving, Bharat requested that Chris examine his ageing grandfather who had fallen off the trail and broken his hip. Several of the family members felt he should be flown to the nearest hospital in Biratnagar 160 km (100 miles) away. The old man refused to go. For one thing, it would mean an arduous and painful carry in a straw basket down more than 300 m (1,000 ft) onto the valley floor, then a 2,400 m (8,000 ft) carry up to the airfield at Tapeljung.

So scarce is skilled medical care in Nepal that he would be considered very lucky by most Nepalis to be able to use the hospital's facilities. In addition, he was wealthy enough to be able to make the journey, a luxury beyond the resources of the average Nepali. But the real reason for not wanting to go was that he simply did not wish to leave his home and family who fussed over him and tended to his every need.

After checking him over, Chris reassured Bharat and his grandfather and worried grandmother that he was receiving the best possible care and attention. Lori and I checked his skin for pressure areas and skin breakdown but his wife had cared for him beautifully. We stressed the importance of him drinking plenty of milk and eating a balanced diet, and we gave him multi-vitamin and mineral supplements. We then bade our farewells. Bharat kissed his grandfather's feet and, weeping openly, left. We were all very moved.

We were now trekking through country that had a high proportion of Limbus, a Mongoloid-type race who have their own distinctive language, music and dance. The women are easily recognised by their elaborate gold necklaces and exquisite nose jewellery, and we would meet them travelling in the opposite direction along the narrow trails. Despite the often heavy loads they were carrying, as soon as they saw us approaching they would step aside politely and wait for us to pass. Feeling as if we were pushing them off the trail I would often automatically say 'thank you' in English, then in

Nepali, 'tapaili kasto cha', a simple greeting akin to 'Howya going mate, awright?' Incredibly, they would roll down the hill in peals of laughter. Lori and I would join in, not wanting to be left out of the joke. Then, three young Limbu women and a man stood waiting for us to pass I repeated my greeting. The man bolted off down the hill and the women screamed with laughter. Bharat and Chris were engrossed in conversation and had fallen behind. When they caught up with us Bharat asked what the joke was. I repeated it once more. 'Why, what's wrong,' I asked. His face turned red. 'Oh no, I can't say, it is very bad.' Judging by the expression on his face, which was about to explode, I insisted. He turned to Chris and gave a gesture with his hand. 'Cherie, I don't know how you managed to do it,' Chris was amused. 'With your Aussie accent it sounded like you were asking the men passing by if they had a hard on!'

Less than one day below Ghunsa, Mingma, who had been Lori's faithful trail companion, became weaker and weaker, finally admitting he could no longer continue. Checking his temperature revealed a startling 104°F, and a bounding pulse. Besides feeling weak, other symptoms were abdominal tenderness, nausea and some vomiting. Not feeling at this point that his condition was serious enough to warrant an evacuation to Kathmandu by helicopter, yet not wanting to take any chances by moving him up to a higher elevation, it was decided that Lori stay with him to monitor his condition and regularly dispense a combination of several potent antibiotics. We would continue on to Ghunsa, taking advantage of the 600 m (2,000 ft) gain in altitude to acclimatise for several days and wait to see what developed. Although the house they stayed in was only two hours from Ghunsa, Lori felt suddenly isolated. Nonetheless she bravely took on the responsibility, fearful that whatever infection he did have could spread to the rest of the household which included a three-month old baby.

Lori told me later, 'Never in my life have I had such an experience. I really felt for the first time how much we take for granted living in the States. These people were so poor, they had nothing. I imagined a situation like this happening without our presence and assistance, the whole family could have just died.' We all know intellectually, but to experience personally the inequity of medical care that exists in the world gives an awareness on an entirely different level. I was really pleased to have had Lori along to share these thoughts.

The contrast went further. During our days in Ghunsa we had been deluged with the various health problems of the 300 inhabitants. Among the many complaints were five or six badly abscessed teeth with the patients begging to have them pulled out. Chris was reluctant to go ahead with extractions for fear of speading the bacteria into the bloodstream and causing a generalised septicaemia. He gave them all a course of antibiotics and promised to extract the offending teeth on his return. Meanwhile, a gentleman Nepali whose home was in a nearby valley and who was trained as a dentist in India, with a practice in Kathmandu, sat by a cosy hearth drinking rakshi and laughing at our efforts. 'Do you honestly think you can make a difference?' he commented. 'This is like throwing salt into the sea, you are simply wasting your time.' What he failed to realise was that what we were doing was as much for ourselves as for the local population. On a personal level, caring made an enormous difference. We still clung to the ethics of the sixties, and as individuals believed we were personally responsible for making the world what it is today.

We all breathed a sigh of relief at signs of Mingma's improvement. Although he was insured, it was debatable whether the government would have authorised a helicopter evacuation, a service usually reserved for foreigners. He may have had to wait a week or more, or maybe one would not have come at all. Our mail runner on K2 had died alone on the trail, delivering letters to our team, and we were well aware how quickly life can be snuffed out in these remote regions. By the morning of the fourth day of his illness, Mingma's temperature was down to 101°F-102°F and he was taking fluids without vomiting. We felt secure enough in taking off for Base Camp and had arranged for his care and convalescence in a more comfortable and larger home in Ghunsa. He managed to walk there the following day. It was another 12 days before he felt strong enough to join us.

One thing at least was working in our favour. Although the temperatures were bitingly cold, there was no snow. Bharat had commented that it had been a particularly dry season which was to our benefit. The only signs of winter were heavy frosts and verglased rocks which made walking tricky. Ghunsa was surrounded by tall, rocky peaks, and frozen waterfalls hung in the ravines.

Early in the morning the village streets were deserted, not a soul stirred. As the first rays of sun hit, as late as ten o'clock, people began to move outside to the wide verandahs and porches, to start the tasks of the day: mending clothes, knitting and weaving. In a week or so the entire village would move to their winter dwellings in Pele 150 m (500 ft) lower down the valley. It was far too cold to spend the entire winter in Ghunsa due to lack of sun. In Pele the rays of the sun reached the dwellings as early as seven in the morning and stayed until four in the afternoon.

Far from trying to attract people to carry for us, we were faced with a difficult selection process. Everyone liked the idea of an attractive cash bonus to help them over the lean winter months, and the journey to Base Camp, far from arduous, was thought of as a fun social event to break the monotony of the winter months. We tried to be as fair as possible, taking a selection from numerous families in order to spread the wealth around a little. Only those who could show they had suitable clothing and footwear, were in good health and not pregnant, were hired. 'That's just what we need, a delivery at 17,000 feet,' I remarked to Lori after turning away a disappointed young girl, seven months pregnant.

The previous weeks had shown Mongol to be a charming companion. Impeccably honest in his dealings, he showed good judgement and gave discreet advice when called for. Once again we found he had advised us well by pointing out that cash, instead of the somewhat inappropriate equipment listed as being required by the government, would be better appreciated. We also assured everyone that there would be mats and tents available for sleeping. Secure in the knowledge that no lives would be lost from exposure, we started up the valley to Base Camp, feeling full of gaiety and laughter.

The object of much joking and hilarity among these openly promiscuous people was the impressive size of Lori's breasts and the fact that we all wore pile clothing with large and obvious zippers that passed underneath the crotch. Their behaviour stood out in stark contrast to their Hindu neighbours. We all felt a bit silly, but were relieved to be distracted from the intensity of our purpose. Mongol and Tirthay had five or six women actively pursuing them, and we joked to Mongol about it. In unexpected seriousness he answered, 'One woman is good enough for me. Three at once is too much big trouble.' They were all competing to share a warm sleeping bag and cook tent with the staff since they knew the food would be better and there would be a kerosene heater to share. The women's aggressiveness in pursuing this end was quite entertaining to watch.

The girl who caught my eye the most was devastatingly beautiful, possessing the finest features and mischievous smile, which was usually directed towards Bharat. Her husband was away on a long visit to Darjeeling. It was not unusual for Sherpa women to have several husbands, just as Hindu men may have several wives, although that practice has now been outlawed. As traders, Sherpa women would be accustomed to long absences, so a family of brothers would often share the same wife. As well as keeping the woman happy, it had the advantage of consolidating property. This girl had only one husband and Bharat told us her nickname among the villagers was 'Lick Lick'. 'That's a nice name,' Chris said.

'I wonder how things worked out last night?' I commented to Chris the following morning as we took down the tents. 'I don't know exactly, but I saw Tirthay down by the stream collecting water and he looked pretty unhappy. It seems he made an arrangement with a girl who was to help him with the kitchen duties and all she did was kick him out of his sleeping bag and laugh at him when he asked for help this morning!' Poor Tirthay. We both smiled at his predicament.

On 28 November we arrived at Base Camp with all supplies intact and a strong feeling of trust and cohesiveness that had developed among our group on the walk-in.

8

I went to see reality
I had to pay to get inside
It was no better than my dreams
but more expensive, being real.

MICHAEL DRANSFIELD

IT HAS BEEN said that the climate in Antarctica is better known and studied than in the Himalayas. This is due to the tremendous size and inaccessibility of the Himalayas. Generally speaking, the climate is dominated by the summer and winter monsoon systems of Asia; a system which heats up air over the land in summer, causing it to rise. Moisture-laden oceanic airs move in from the sea and release their load under appropriate conditions. In winter, the Asiatic land mass is much colder than the adjoining seas and becomes an intense high pressure system. A general air flow occurs at low levels from south to north, as maritime airs from the Indian Ocean in summer months, and north to south in winter months from the Asiatic mainland. In the upper levels the winds are generally strong easterly in summer and even stronger westerly in winter.

This being our understanding, we anticipated our north face route may have some troublesome problems with wind, though this was probably an over-simplification. Adrian Burgess, with his considerable experience of winter Himalayan climbing, said that northerly winds never seem to last for many days. When they did change direction, it was often preceded by one day of calm weather. In addition, we were to learn that the Himalayas are affected by extra tropical weather systems that move over the north of the sub-continent from west to east in winter. On an average, we could expect six to seven 'western disturbances' every month.

Although the eastern Himalaya has a prolonged monsoon season from June to October, the winter would bring very little snow with these western disturbances. By contrast, the western Himalaya, which experiences a much drier summer monsoon, would expect a longer, colder winter, with more snow. For instance, the snow line in the west drops to 1,500 m (5,000 ft), whereas in the eastern Himalaya it is more commonly 3,000 m (10,000 ft) and above. Geographically, Kanchenjunga stood in a prime location for its first winter attempt, with predictably less snow and warmer temperatures.

For all our research on winter weather in the Himalayas, the fabled jetstream winds dominated our thinking. They are called 'killer winds', with reported velocities exceeding 200 km (125 miles) per hour. In warmer months these winds usually linger at around 9,000 m (30,000 ft) and above to drop down occasionally to around 8,500 m (28,000 ft). In winter, the frequency and duration of these 'dips' in the jetstream increase markedly. Above 6,300 m (21,000 ft) this becomes of increasing significance and concern to the climber.

These winds are recognised as being generally westerlies, but again we were cautioned by Adrian Burgess. Thought should be given, he said, to considerable deviations caused by local influences: 'Routes that pass through or near cols are generally more windy and can funnel winds onto the slopes normally considered in the ice.' 'You mean like where our route runs right by the north col?' I asked Chris, but already I knew the answer. Sir John Hunt's description of weather on Everest stayed in my mind. 'In winter, the great westerly wind rules supreme in these high and lonely places.'

The porters were paid off and fled like frightened deer into the valley below. The sun disappeared behind Ramthang Chang (Wedge Peak) yet it was scarcely two in the afternoon. The cold hit with a stunning blow and we momentarily reeled under its impact. Using movement as a cure for our innermost fears and shaking aside childlike feelings of abandonment, we set up tents in a rough circle, anticipating the necessity for having as few steps as possible from cook tent to sleeping tent in the event of a heavy storm. A vacuum had been created by the departure of our happy companions, and the rituals and routine of setting up camp helped to fill it.

The air was still and clear. Kanchenjunga had never looked so beautiful. Scoured by furious winds that had torn apart her mantle of snow, she stood naked and inviting; glistening with the shimmering blue of hard ice in the fading rays of winter sun. It was 28 November 1984.

'It doesn't look like there's an inch of snow left on the mountain. It's quite amazing.' I lay huddled beside Chris in our lightweight qualofil bags. We planned to save our heavy duty, down bags for higher on the mountain and colder temperatures, for it was necessary not only to acclimatise to the altitude but also to the intense cold. 'Yeah, I didn't expect it to look quite like that,' Chris confided. 'But remember, Bharat did say it had been exceptionally dry.'

In some respects this was an unexpected bonus, for although winter ice climbing is considered more difficult and dangerous, it is also much more enjoyable, since the climber has to rely entirely on his or her own skills rather than deal with the unpredictable moods of the mountain with its soft snow or slab avalanches. Apart from being incredibly boring plugging steps through deep snow, there is little skill involved other than exercising judgement in whether the risks make it worth continuing or not.

The first three days were spent acclimatising and organising Base Camp. The weather during this time remained remarkably clear and we were impatient to take advantage of it. However, realising the importance of pacing oneself for adequate acclimatisation, we held in check these impulsive urges to 'rush' the mountain. In three carries by Mongol, Chris and myself, Camp 1 was used as a temporary dump site at 5,500 m (18,500 ft) and now stood fully stocked.

On the morning of 5 December we set out to put the route through to Camp 2. I was picking my way through the moraine when a giant boulder came loose and trapped my leg. A blood-curdling cry escaped from my lips as Chris and Mongol looked on in horror. I was unable to move an inch. In dismay I saw my chances of climbing the mountain evaporate in seconds before my eyes, replaced by the vision of a crushed leg. Not until this moment did I fully realise how much I wanted to climb Kanchenjunga. To be cut off at a mere 5,500 m (18,500 ft) was more than I could bear.

Using the shafts of both ice axes as levers, Chris and Mongol were able to move the boulder just enough to free my leg. The soft tissue of the calf and lower leg was badly bruised. I felt a strong burning pain, but realised immediately there was no suspicious deep ache indicating a broken bone. I was overjoyed to be given another chance. Mollified, I hobbled back to camp alone, laughing to myself. The thought of a crushed leg was trivial compared to the disappointment of not being able to continue. With rest the leg would be fine, and it took its place along with my knee and shoulder as injuries not to be ignored but limbs to be gently coerced into performing to absolute maximum capability.

Whilst I greedily ate up the beauty and solitude of the surroundings as a bona fide convalescent, Chris and Mongol put up the route and carried several loads to Camp 2. On Chris's return I showed him with delight tracks measuring about 7.5 cm (3 in) across belonging to what I guessed to be a fair-sized cat — either snow leopard or lynx — that had passed by an area of sandy loam close to our campsite. The snow leopard has large feet and possesses a magnificent fluffy pelt and long bushy tail. It counts as one of the main predators of the Himalayas, covering an immense range from 2,000 m (6,500 ft) to over 5,000 m (16,500 ft). I wondered if his larder was the herd of goats still grazing on the pastures at Pang Pema. The snow leopard, which has never been very common, is now considered a rarity.

Another more likely candidate responsible for the tracks was the lynx, known for frequenting extreme altitudes. It is recognised by its short tail and black-tipped ears, yet because of its extremely shy nature, encounters are rare. Its diet of small rodents, marmots and birds could have explained its presence here. Although the pattern of tracks changed over several days, we were never lucky enough to solve the identity of our mystery visitor.

We were both excited by our progress; in six days we had already established Camp 2. Mongol returned to Base Camp and we celebrated with a rest day. Chris explained how he had chosen a different route from 1981 in order to circumnavigate the large number of wide crevasses which, because of lack of snow, he anticipated difficulty in passing. Instead, our route would hug the northern flank of the glacier, passing under Gimmigela (the Twins) to reach Camp 2 via two ice gullies. The route was rather steep, 45-50 degrees of black water ice, and exceptionally hard for the crampons to bite into due to the extremely low temperatures.

Mongol, although somewhat slow and hesitant, had managed the difficulties and Chris was guardedly optimistic about his climbing abilities. All he needed was more practice. It was normal for Sherpas to learn their climbing skills in this manner in an area such as the Himalayas, which most mountaineers would consider the peak of their climbing experience. How else could they learn their trade? What was different about our trip was the total absence of any fixed line rope which is normally left in place over the most difficult sections. It is a considerable safeguard for the inexperienced, exhausted or injured climber. Some Sherpas climb for their entire careers never knowing how to set up a belay or climb safely without fixed lines. Chris and I enjoyed the challenge of teaching Mongol the crucial difference between a climber and a load carrier on fixed lines. We were grateful for his eagerness to learn and help carry loads.

Time was a critical element in the ultimate success of reaching the summit, and every good day of weather had to be maximised. The new route was shorter and more direct. It was, however, more difficult and falling rocks did present some problems. Chris looked forward to me checking it out to see whether I thought the advantages outweighed the risks.

On 12 December I wrote in my diary: 'We've been on the mountain 12 days now. How can I describe what climbing "Kanche" in winter is like? In the background is a constant roar, terrifying in its simple persistence. Sometimes I imagine I'm standing in a dark tunnel, waiting the approach of a freight train from which there is no escape. At other times I see the thundering power of Niagara Falls. But the postcards always picture a cement sidewalk and handrail for tourists, and trains were made by man. It has a facade of civility. This is too crude, too raw a power for any such comparisons, and we dare not tamper with it.

'Mostly the winds have been from the west, and then they shift to a more south westerly direction. Theoretically we should be

ABOVE: *Mongol Singh Tamang, 24 years old; Dr Chris Chandler, 36 years old; and Cherie Bremer-Kamp, 38 years old, make up our small team.*

BELOW: *The route shown by ——— is our 1981 climb up Yalung Kang. The route shown by ········· is our 1985 climb up Kanchenjunga. Ascent bivouacs are marked with a ▲ and descent bivouacs are marked with a ●.*

Kanchenjunga
Summit

Yalung Kang

Bivouac

Bivouac

Bivouac

Camp 4

Bivouac

Camp 3

Camp 2

protected, but every so often the torrent spills over unleashing its
fury upon us. A subtle but unmistakable change of sound warns us
several seconds ahead of its approach and we brace the tent, tense
with readiness. Soon we are pinned down by the force, clinging
with all our strength to the structure that makes up our protective
nylon womb. Ten, twenty seconds elapse. Finally it passes and we
are able to rest before the next onslaught. Yet this is a mere taste of
the fury going on above. God help us if we are caught in such a
wind.'

Our progress to date had been encouraging. Camp 2 was completely stocked, and a route put through the first icefall. Once again
I acknowledged the familiar dread of climbing through these gates
of hell that led to the summit — towering cliffs of ice that had the
power to snuff out life at any given moment in time. Still I
questioned why we chose to tread such a path. When the boulder
rolled on my leg the feeling of utter dismay, of being cheated from
being able to continue, overwhelmed me. The depth and power of
that inner desire surprised me when I encountered it.

Now my back and neck were fine, I had stopped taking the
drugs, my bruised leg was working OK and I had finally discarded
the splint. It kept on sliding down my leg as it was made for a
Cherie 10 kg (20 lb) heavier. No matter; I forgot all about my knee
when climbing as it suffered far less stress than when I was walking
over the icy boulders of the moraine.

On 15 December the continuing high winds forced us to drop
down to Base Camp. It proved to be quite an ordeal because of the
frigid temperatures and hurricane force winds. My crampons came
loose twice during the steep, ice gully descent. Fitting them on
again in such an exposed situation, between blasts by the wind
which tore down the gully at a furious rate, is a memory I'll not
soon forget. The three of us were roped together. I was first,
Mongol was in the middle and Chris was coming down last.

Mongol still had much to learn about rope handling; as soon as
he was over the difficulties he took off down the gentle slope
forgetting that Chris was not able to follow at the same speed.

*Lonak figures as an especially holy place in Buddhist mythology. Tranquil, green
pastures lend a stark contrast to the rugged mountain surroundings.*

Taken by surprise, before I could yell a warning, the rope pulled taut and Chris was yanked from his delicate stance to fall and slide about 15 m (50 ft) down the slope. Bruised and sore, but not seriously hurt, Chris was furious at Mongol's carelessness. His reaction was justified, after all. It was a lesson Mongol should never forget. We were lucky the outcome was not more serious. However, Chris could not contain his anger and it developed into a long string of verbal abuse.

A deepening irritation had been growing towards Mongol. For one thing his presence in the tent made it cramped and eliminated any privacy we might share. In addition, Chris felt, as did I, that Mongol never did anything unless we asked him to. He would quite happily lie motionless in the sleeping bag while we collected snow for melting, adjusted the ropes that held the fly over the tent in place or cooked meal after meal which he happily ate. I had reasoned with Chris that as this was his first time in such a situation he needed guidance as to what was expected of him, and having just been promoted from cook he naturally didn't want to go back to that role. Besides, I never minded fixing the meals. Going outside for any reason other than to climb was my pet hate; I would try to avoid it at any cost.

Now all these suppressed feelings of resentment came pouring out and Mongol, crushed by the criticism, lowered his head and began to cry. I felt Chris was going too far and found myself identifying with Mongol. I put my arm round him and tried to cheer him up. 'Its a tough way to learn a lesson, but you won't ever forget it will you?'

We unroped and quietly packed away the gear. Chris was withdrawn, realising I was telling him in my own way that he'd gone too far and he knew it himself. He stayed back as though he needed time alone to think and collect himself. Mongol and I were sitting at the base of the first ice step in a place where we traditionally removed crampons and overboots, had a bite to eat and drink, and generally rested. The sun was trying to come out and we seemed to be protected from the wind.

Chris, above us and still climbing down, was having a problem with one of his crampons. It slipped off and he fell a short distance. He was angry again that the crampons were being so troublesome and he felt that Mongol and I were watching with wide smirks on our faces. He began climbing down the remaining section, a short 3 m (10 ft) vertical step of ice. Striking a resounding blow with the axe, it bit into the ice and he lunged over the side in an action that looked almost as if it was filled with despair. The ice was unforgiving and Chris came crashing down, to land a few feet away. I knew he had hurt himself badly, but couldn't get close enough for the kicking and thrashing of his arms and legs. 'Mongol, get my first aid kit. Chris will you stop that so I can at least see if you're hurt?' He was soon cradled in my arms. 'You numbskull, of course we weren't laughing at you. Here, keep still and let me clean up your elbow.' There was a deep laceration on his left elbow which I knew needed suturing. Two bandaids tucked the protruding sub-cutaneous tissue back into place.

Mongol took off down the moraine and we slowly made our way back to Base Camp, relieved to be on our own. I wondered what Mongol thought of the antics of his employers, but put the thought aside. I really didn't care. All I cared about was Chris and my love poured out to him for I knew he was suffering deeply. This was his first outburst since San Francisco. I wished I could take away some of his agony. I was pretty shaken up inside, and knew that it could have been dangerous. Another side of me was relieved that this release of emotion hadn't been directed at me.

Tirthay was a wonderful cook and the mess tent was kept clean and well organised. The kerosene heater provided delicious warmth and bathed the tent in a soft, golden light. We gathered around it as a centre for social exchange and the cosy atmosphere did wonders for our spirits. As soon as we arrived, the storm that had sent us scurrying down the mountain passed and the weather turned good. We accepted the irony and relaxed and enjoyed three days of rest.

At Camp 2 we only saw two hours of sun a day. The rest of the time the entire north side of the mountain was in a shadow. By comparison, Base Camp was like a tropical island. Wandering about in shorts and long underwear, I marvelled at the body's ability to adapt to cold. I laughed when I remembered how we complained of the cold even as low as Ghunsa. Lori, who had been in her heavy, down sleeping bag since 3,300 m (11,000 ft) even had times where she would forgo her down pants and jacket during the day and simply wear her pile gear. It was not getting warmer, quite the opposite, but our bodies were adjusting to the cold.

Lori was settling down into the routine nicely and everyone enjoyed her company. Her idea of 'exposure' was walking the gentle slopes behind Base Camp. She confided to me that one time she froze with fright in one spot, unable to move until Tirthay arrived and helped her down. We both agreed she should always go walking with a companion.

Now it was a week before Christmas and colder temperatures still lay ahead. I washed my hair, for we all had head lice. The hair froze immediately. I was satisfied — freezing the little buggers should stop them for a while I thought. My feet had suffered most from the cold. They had spent too many hours a day without feeling. Already the big toenails had turned purple. Was it worth losing part of a big toe? I suppose so, but nothing more. Chris's arm was healing up fine. I was surprised that the bandaids had worked so well in holding together such a deep laceration.

We took off for Camp 2 on 19 December. This time we took our full down sleeping bags plus extra rations of yak butter, fresh garlic and rakshi. We elected to climb without ropes on this lower section. It was quicker and we all felt comfortable, including Mongol, in moving over the steep terrain that was now so familiar. The route via the ice gullies was proving to be quicker and more direct but as Chris had predicted, rock fall was a problem. A loud whirring sound, like the beating wings of a helicopter, or at other times a sharp twang like a bullet from a shotgun, would warn us of impending danger.

Gasping for air I stood watching as one of these missiles made directly for Chris, who was delicately balanced on the front points of his crampons. It all happened so quickly. I remember calling out 'rock' and Chris, electrified with anticipation, fell forward into the slope, gripping the ice axe and hammer. A millisecond later the rock tore into his pack. It was an unpleasantly close shave.

At 12.30 pm we sat resting in the sun on our 'lunch rock' nibbling on cheese and crackers, sipping Tang and studying the thin wisps of high cloud that were flying past in the otherwise clear blue sky. By 2 pm we were leaning with the full weight of our bodies into the wind. The tent, only 60 m (200 ft) away, was scarcely visible in the swirling snow. I was glad for my neoprene face mask and one-piece down suit. At least the crampons had stayed in place. Putting them on in the sun or the warmth of a tent, rather than in the frigid temperatures of a blizzard, seemed to be a critical factor in getting a meticulously snug fit. Neither of us could recall having had such a problem with crampons before.

Over the next seven days we managed two carries to just below 7,000 m (23,000 ft) and our desired campsite. Each time, deteriorating weather forced us to retreat prematurely. The weather in general showed a marked decline. We had missed the optimum period to be climbing, and now we lay stalemated by continuous high winds that held captive the entire upper section of the mountain down to 7,000 m (23,000 ft). It shifted back and forth from west to south west and back again, but always from the same general direction. We soon stopped anticipating a change to the north. It never happened. What I did wonder was whether it would drop lower and completely envelop Camp 2, since sometimes it did drop low enough to include the north col. Surviving in such a wind seemed out of the question; here we were playing a game with a deadly companion.

Sometimes the wind would release its grip on the mountain to yield 300 m (1,000 ft) or so, and cautiously we would creep upwards only to come running back down again to the safety of our tent. Chastened by our experience, I wondered if the lull in the wind had just been an illusion. Although not hampered by deep snow, moving upwards had been slower than we would have liked. Perhaps we needed to acclimatise more?

I also noticed the intense cold making me weaker and more breathless. When the gusts of wind came, I felt myself fighting for air. It was as though the passage of wind created an enormous vacuum and sucked all the available oxygen with it. A feeling of panic subsided with the wind's departure. Chris had remarked on a similar feeling.

Christmas was celebrated with me fixing a special 'Christmas' omelette and then Chris making us cups of 'Christmas' hot chocolate. It was served with much fanfare and ceremony. Mongol was puzzled as he looked at the food, it tasted the same as every other breakfast to him.

On 27 December Mongol returned to Base Camp. I think he had tired of our imaginary feasts of barbequed goat, hot fresh bread and fresh salad. He wanted the real thing. I, too, was despondent. With every passing day I saw the chances of our climbing the mountain slipping like sand through our fingers. It seemed as if we were wasting our time. Hadn't we been patient enough? The mountain had yielded nothing. We had given it a sterling effort, I reasoned. Besides, we had K2 to look forward to in the summer, although my feet would be lucky to recover by then.

Chris turned to me. Amidst the piles of down, the only thing exposed was his nose. 'Why not play the waiting game just a little longer. I've got a feeling there's going to be a break in the weather around the middle of January. We've already invested so much in the mountain, to give up now ... Well, you remember how we felt turning around on Yalung Kang.' 'I suppose you're right, I agreed. 'There can be no harm sticking around another couple of weeks. If we wait long enough we'll start meeting the spring expeditions. What are we going to do with Mongol?'

This topic had been a continuing source of discussion between us. It was obvious that he very much wanted to go to the summit with us. The fact there was no fixed line and therefore no easy way off the mountain should he decide to return, was a point of concern. Now that he had helped us establish Camp 2 and carry loads part way to Camp 3, he seemed to become more deadweight that we could discard.

As his employers we had every right to send him back, and some may say a responsibility to do this given his lack of experience. Yet he was capable of descending solo a 45–50 degree ice gully, which revealed a good measure of his skill and confidence. He seemed to have a fair enough understanding of what he was taking on, and the risks involved. He had seen his Sherpa friends suffer from frost-bitten fingers and feet that had to be amputated, and had many friends who had not returned from expeditions.

I suppose what concerned me most was Bharat's involvement. He actively and vigorously encouraged Mongol to accompany us, and due to language difficulties I could not ascertain how this ultimately influenced his decision. Bharat was aggressive as Mongol's advocate. He stressed that because Mongol had helped us establish Camp 3 he had a right, which we couldn't refuse, to go for the summit. This of course was utter nonsense. It is true that a rule does exist which says that if a high altitude porter makes a carry to the highest camp on the mountain, he must be allowed the choice by his leader to go for the summit.

The 'highest camp' referred to in the rules is a tent at probably around 8,000 m (27,000 ft) with a fixed line leading from Base Camp to the highest camp, and more than likely well stocked with food and oxygen bottles. We thought that above Camp 3 we would have no more tents, only bivouacs. To have to suffer Bharat's interference based on an uninformed opinion was quite distracting, although I recognised that he felt he was acting in Mongol's best interest. We decided to ask Mongol himself. I dreaded him saying yes. I really missed being alone with Chris on the mountain, and thought Chris did too.

Stormbound in our tents for another four days, we were surprised that barely an inch of snow settled. 'With the force of that wind, it's a wonder we get any snow at all,' Chris remarked. Mongol had returned and, as expected, immediately accepted Chris's offer to accompany us. On 31 December a partial break in the weather occurred. The skies were still heavily overcast as we roused from sleeping bags at 4.30 am to start the endless task of making brews. The gusts of wind seemed to be lessening as night turned to early morning, the only sign we needed to start our hopes soaring.

It was a pain in the neck having only one spoon left, all the others had snapped in half from the cold. Two of the posts on Chris's crampons had also broken off, presumably from the cold, and this morning as he tightened the straps another one broke off. They had been purchased new for the trip and were made of the highest quality tensile steel. As we had no thermometer we could only hazard a guess at how low the temperatures had dropped. 'What are you going to do now?' I was dismayed. 'Just use more straps to keep the suckers on,' he replied with resignation. As if to reinforce the point that it was cold, the post on Mongol's crampon also broke off.

This was now our third time through the upper ice gully. We had rappelled down but left 45 m (150 ft) of line and several pickets in place. All we had to do was free climb the lower section to the base of the rope, quickly jumar up to the last anchor point and steepest section and then climb the remaining pitch that would lead to the first snow terrace. We had stopped using a rope to cross the crevasse-strewn glacier. The snow was so hard that our crampons barely left an indentation; the chances of falling into a crevasse were close to zero.

Moving without a rope gave us a tremendous feeling of mobility and freedom and we made good time, in spite of the periodic blasts we got from ice crystals funnelling down the gully from the upper mountain. At least the ice cliffs towering above us seemed to be less active during these winter months — small comfort as I tried to stomp life back into my frozen feet.

'Come on Mongol, don't take so long,' I screamed silently. The soles of my feet were 'gone' and my hands would go through periods of wanting to 'freeze'. I recognised the moment with a feeling of panic. The best cure was to remove the outer mitts and place the icy paws against the closest, warm bare skin: namely Chris's neck which he would good naturedly offer. Occasionally I was able to return the favour. Then again we both practised *tumo*, visualising the blood vessels as rivers of fire bringing warmth to our hands and feet.

Chris led the last pitch out of the gully, but not before the tip of the pick to his Choinard ice hammer snapped off, making it useless. We passed mine back and forth between the two of us. Heavy clouds continued to move rapidly across the sky but we ignored them. A momentum was growing that would be difficult to arrest. We picked up our cached supplies and moved out onto the great snow terrace. 'This was what I was afraid of.' The look on Chris's face registered disgust. The whole slope gave off a hollow-sounding echo as Chris knocked his ice axe against it. It gave me a

ABOVE: *Food, prepackaged in America, is carefully weighed in uniform bundles and divided into high altitude and low altitude rations.*

BELOW: *A well run kitchen and a smiling face are invaluable aids to boost our morale on this extended winter expedition. Not only was Tirthay a meticulous cook but he had unending patience. (Photo Lori Orlando)*

OVERLEAF: *The beginning of the first icefall, altitude 5,700 m (19,000 ft).*

very leery feeling. We hoped the cold temperatures would prevent it from sloughing off. Gingerly we made our way across it, for what was there to do but move onward and upward?

It was now 2 pm and we had arrived at the old Czech campsite. Feet had frozen. 'Gotta warm up, get a brew going,' was a thought we shared wordlessly. With shovels in hand we spanned the surrounding area looking for a suitable site for a snow cave. The deepest we could excavate in the hard snow was 0.6 m (2 ft) before hitting the blue ice of the glacier.

We tried again and again, searching for places where the blown snow may have collected in sufficient amounts to provide a place where we could dig a small shelter. There was nothing but ice in every direction. Time was running out, we needed to move fast, yet I found myself staring at objects as though hypnotised. It was difficult to break out of the trance. I noticed Mongol was doing the same. The situation was rapidly becoming serious. Finally Chris yelled down from the slopes above, 'Hey, I think I've found our old bookshelf bivvy!' 'You sweetheart,' I thought, and we stiffly moved on upwards to the site.

There was no ceiling, but in desperation we climbed down into it anyway. Surrounded on either side by walls of ice 3 m (10 ft) high, we were at last protected from the main force of the wind. After hours of searching and then digging out the floor so that it was wide enough for us to lie down, we stuffed our packs into the most open side, attempting to block the blasts of wind and snow that found a path to our hideaway. The crevasse was less than 0.9 m (3 ft) wide and 3 m (10 ft) long. Four hours had passed since we first stopped and we at last crawled into our down bags and sacs to seek warmth and rest.

ABOVE: *Balanced delicately on front points which barely bite into the blackwater ice, Mongol braces himself against storm force winds which blast the gully and bring flying missiles of rock and ice.*

BELOW: *A sudden gust of wind which has spilt over the north east col announces its arrival with a thunderous roar.*

PREVIOUS PAGE: *Our Camp 2 was in the lee of prevailing winds and low enough to be protected from the full force of jetstream winds which in winter months could drop to as low as 6,600–7,000 m (22,000–23,000 ft). As a result, any upward movement was halted for days on end.*

It had been 12 hours since we ate or drank and we now began the painfully slow process of melting snow. The gas stove gave off about as much heat as a candle. Finally Chris handed me a cup of precious warm fluid. 'Happy Birthday, sweetie.' I detected a wide grin under his icy beard. It was my 39th birthday, and New Year's Eve. We all took turns in melting snow late into the night. My feet began to thaw. I was surprised how warm I felt. Blasted by waves of spindrift, we drifted off into an exhausted sleep, awakened only occasionally by drips of moisture. Capsules of condensation caused by my breath would slither their way through the catacomb of layers finally to reach the exquisite warmth of skin, their ultimate goal. The arrival was signalled by my startled arousal.

I peeked out to check the weather. The wind remained moderate, the sky was black and starry — just the break we needed. It was now 5 am and my bladder had reached critical capacity. Unfortunately, it not only required boots, overboots, crampons and full dress, but time to execute the manoeuvre. Chris saved an impending disaster by suggesting I just pick up the insulated pad and pee under that. I found there was more snow on top of the pad than underneath, but it worked and I was grateful. I then cast a concerned eye in Mongol's direction, out of modesty. But where was he? I saw only a mound of snow in the place where he had fallen asleep. 'My God. He must have died during the night.' I was filled with crippling guilt. Careful examination showed the mound of snow mimicking the slow, rhythmic movement of his breath. I was relieved.

I then took another look outside. My heart sank, and this time it was no false alarm. The jetstream had enclosed its grip around Kanchenjunga and Yalung Kang to below 7,800 m (26,000 ft). The lower level of the wind was encroaching uncomfortably close to the territory we now occupied. I was being blasted by swirling gusts of blinding particles of snow. We had both witnessed the jetstream drop down to where we stood now at 7,000 m (23,000 ft) in no time at all. Chris's and my emergency lights switched on simultaneously telling us to 'evacuate'.

It was a good thing we drank last night as there was no time now. What a struggle to put on boots, overboots and crampons in such a confined space, and pack away gear that was frozen stiff with a thick coating of ice. Then we had to organise gear to be cached. Chris had to warn Mongol that if he didn't hurry up he would be left behind before the message penetrated that the situation was critical. In little over half an hour we were stumbling down blindly in the direction of the icefall.

Three quick rappels through the ice gully and we were back at Camp 2 in probably close to two hours. Our sleeping bags looked like dried-up prunes. The pile gear was stiff and frozen solid. Uncared for, the tent looked more like an ice cave than anything else, but it was better than a crevasse and we crawled in gratefully.

Twenty-four hours later, with no sign of the storm abating, we made off for Base Camp to dry out. It had been a late start and already it was after 12 noon. Chris wanted Mongol to melt fluids and cook breakfast and consequently none of us had much to drink. Foolishly I had given my ration of Tang to Chris without thinking. After all we'd be in Base Camp in a few hours. I usually took my time on the moraine guarding my knee protectively against a sudden slip on the icy boulders, but today I was excessively slow. I felt quite weak and drained of energy. Mongol had taken off and we watched him disappear into the distance.

I realised too late that I was suffering from dehydration and as the stoves were cached, there was nothing I could do but methodically plod on. I knew I would get there; I also knew Chris was starting to get impatient with me and it was deepening into irritation. I reminded him that because of a woman's physiology she succumbed more easily to the effects of dehydration, and reasoned with him to be patient or go on without me. I was following in Chris's footsteps, drawn along by the momentum of his movement.

We both missed the turnoff to Base Camp, fog from the valley moved in and for a moment we were disorientated. Tension mounted in Chris. I tried to be cool and joked about it. Chris was in no mood and with dread I recognised the signs of what would happen.

Back on the right trail again I still moved no quicker since I felt dragged down by an incredible weight. The anger in Chris grew. It was just before dark and the final 150 m (500 ft) climb to Base Camp remained. I'd taken off my pack to rest when the blows started raining down on my head and back. Then he threw the pack and the ice axe at me. The axe missed and hit a nearby rock which sparkled in the night. 'So, what are you going to do now, kill yourself because I'm such a monster?' He got up and disappeared into the shadows. After a while I picked up my pack and ice axe and continued on to Base Camp.

Everyone was puzzled and concerned about our late arrival. I managed to say a few words about not feeling good, drank some tea and went to the tent. Chris was sitting alone in the darkness. Without exchanging words I slipped into the bag and wept silently. I thought he would come to me but it was clear he was still holding on to his anger. My heart was pounding so hard I thought it would burst through my chest. I felt so deeply shamed, sorrow and despair overwhelmed me. Screaming, crying, laughing — nothing would alter what had happened tonight, or all the other times. I had to control the pounding in my chest and neck.

I reached out for the medical kit. I remembered an unopened bottle of 10 mg Valium. There were 60 tablets inside. Good. With that dose I should be careful about depressing my respirations, but what did I care? I popped two, and as an afterthought took another one. I lay down with the bottle beside me and waited a few minutes. Still no effect. I swallowed a few more. It's got to get better soon, I can't stand it much longer. But I really wanted to hang on if I could. Bargaining with myself, I realised I owed more to my children than to take the whole bottle. I settled on a plan, a sort of compromise. I'd take one or two every hour or so until either I felt better, he said he was sorry, or I drifted off into a long sleep. It was decided.

Gradually, imperceptibly, the drug started taking effect. I noticed I was still breathing. Had I been in a normal state I probably would have slept for a week, but I was far from normal. I only felt a slight easing off and some degree of detachment from my emotions. Their voracity had been calmed just enough, but the despair remained. Only feeling Chris's love could take that away, but he lay motionless on the other side of the tent. I stayed awake most of the night going over the long train of events that had brought me to this situation. Occasionally I would drift off into a light sleep suddenly to awake feeling a dreadful pounding in my chest. Overcome with emotion, I would roll over and swallow another pill, depending on how bad I felt.

Tirthay's smiling, concerned face brought tea to our tent door early the next morning. I drank a cup and turned over to lose myself among the covers. I couldn't bear to meet anyone's eyes. Chris got dressed and left the tent. I drifted back to sleep, watching the endless reels of film from my mind. Mid-morning I got up to empty my bladder. Chris was doing tasks around the campsite. 'Oh, I see you've finally decided to get up, fuck-face.' I winced, for he'd said it in front of everyone. They all seemed to be staring at me. I escaped to the safety of the tent and several more Valium, but I couldn't drown the echo of his words.

Lori brought me in a polybottle full of tea. I mumbled a thank you and turned my back. One of the tent poles had broken in the strong winds and Chris was helping her fix it. I could hear them laughing together. It all sounded so normal. When they were finished he came over to the tent door, 'Lori went to the trouble of fixing you some tea and you don't even have the courtesy to drink it. How long are you going to stay there. Your face looks terrible.' 'Until you say you're sorry.' He threw the polybottle at me and left. It was now lunchtime and he came in again. 'Are you going to eat?' 'No.' 'What are you going to do then?' 'Stay here and let you and Mongol climb the mountain, I've had enough.'

I rolled over and turned my back on him. Before I could stop it, the fatal words were out. I was desperately afraid he would turn around once more in anger and leave for the summit. I didn't trust Mongol climbing with Chris. Chris needed me as a safe climbing companion, if nothing else. I felt as though I was abandoning him. But it was true, I had had enough. What would happen, there was only silence as an answer? Ten thousand lifetimes sped through my mind in a single second of time.

I felt him touch the hair on the back of my neck, gently parting it, and then I felt the pressure of his lips. The hair stood on end as my body charged with electricity. I turned and pulled him close to me. Already he had penetrated my inner being, and I pulsated with joy.

From 2–6 January, continuing high winds and storms kept us at Base Camp. The expedition had stalled, and we floated in limbo.

For a time nothing seemed real, the routine tasks around camp were all that gave life tangible form. Several times I was aware of Chris and I standing looking at each other as if struck by an apparition, asking who are we and what are we doing? I began to appreciate more deeply the hardships being endured on our behalf by the good people round us.

The ferocity of the wind didn't seem too different from Camp 2, although I guess the sheer size of our cook tent, large enough for four people to stand in, helped to give that impression. Having no 'aerodynamic' lines, and being so high from the ground, it quivered and shook in an alarming manner, threatening to burst apart at the seams at any moment. Nobody except Chris and I paid the least attention to it and I gathered from the matter of fact way everyone went about their activities, it was normal. We all had a strong interest in preserving the tent intact for it contributed considerably to the quality of life. A broken tent pole was reinforced, the tie-down points strengthened or replaced. The zipper to the door had broken and we shut it on a permanent basis. Mosquitoes did not seem to pose a likely problem, so we cut out the screen and used the windows as a new door. Mealtimes were as rough as a storm at sea, and we were tossed back and forth by the billowing sides of the tent.

Gradually, as I started to participate in activities around Base Camp, life began to feel more normal. Lori was hungry for company other than Tirthay, Bharat and Mingma, and eagerly sought me out to discuss everything from the black soot that came out of her nose when she blew it, to nursing and living in Saudi Arabia. Lori also explained to Chris and me that she was concerned that she had started coughing up sputum that was tinged with black. She thought her lungs were full of soot caused by the kerosene stove. Chris and I reassured her that it was probably due to a post-nasal drip. The soot collecting in her nasal passages was most likely draining down into the back of her throat.

Chris and I had noticed a similar problem with blood-stained sputum. This was of particular concern as it could signal the presence of pulmonary oedema. Clearing the sinuses, which were thick with blood-stained secretions, made us think that the blood was not from our lungs but from dried out sinuses caused by the excessively cold temperatures. We all checked each others' chests, listening with stethoscopes, and they appeared to be clear. We showed no other signs, such as shortness of breath, apart from the ever-present hacking cough — a persistent companion to the high altitude climber. Chris's cough was worse than mine, and I scolded him for smoking, which hardly helped the problem.

Bharat seemed lonely and remote, and he tried to satisfy his intellect by asking questions and giving encouragement and advice on the progress, or more precisely lack of progress, on the mountain. His poetic side saw Chris and me as Shiva and Parbati, romping in play with one another in the high, eternal snows. Mingma gave us daily weather forecasts. 'Sun too sleepy today. Big daddy wind come out and play.' Tirthay, the sweetest and dearest of all, worked tirelessly from sunrise to late at night with kitchen chores. The constant flow of tasty and well-prepared meals slowly restored our bodies and spirits.

Chris and I examined my toes with increasing concern. 'Are you sure you think it's worth it?' His voice was full of love and concern. 'They certainly don't look good, but I suppose I'll give it a chance,' I said with a certain amount of resignation.

We planned to leave the next day, 7 January, and spend the time at Camp 2 waiting for a break in the weather. Chris stood by the medical kit holding up a vial of Dexamethasone, a medication thought to be useful in the treatment of cerebral oedema. 'What do you think, Cherie, shall we throw it in?' I was surprised. 'Do you really think we will need it at this stage? This will be the fourth time we have been to 23,000 feet. We've never taken it on any previous trips.' He hesitated for a moment, then lay it aside. 'Yeah, I guess so. It would probably freeze in the syringe before we had a chance to give it anyway.' We spent the rest of the day mending and checking out worn equipment and sharpening up the points of our ice axes and crampons.

It was 6.30 am. Everyone had assembled outside to bid farewell in the biting cold. We loaded up and parted with hugs and wishes of good luck, success and safety. Once more the familiar track of moraine passed underfoot. I turned to Chris, 'You know it's crazy how every time I go up the glacier, I see splashes of blood over all the boulders. It seems at times almost to blend with the lichen, but when I look again, there's no lichen on the rock at all.' 'Yeah, I remember you mentioning it at the beginning of the trip,' Chris commented. 'I wonder if you are seeing retinal haemorrhages in your peripheral vision. I doubt it, as they are usually without symptoms, but sometimes if bad enough they can cause blindness.' 'It's probably an omen of some kind, warning us of the bloody messes we'll be when we get off this mountain,' I added. We both laughed.

Installed at Camp 2 for four nights and three days of high winds and generally unclimbable weather, we found it more exhausting to be holed up in a small tent than to be out climbing. The morning of 8 January I awoke, or more accurately, rose to a higher level of consciousness, after being blasted for the second night in a row by winds exceeding 160 km/h (100 mph). Drifting in and out of semi-consciousness I would realise the tent was gyrating as if in a wild and macabre ritual dance. 'Thank God for modern techno-logy,' I'd think, gradually easing the load from my face in an attempt to support the structure in the shape it was originally intended.

Holding on to the precious tent poles that kept our fragile world together, I would try to comfort myself with comparisons of a storm in the middle of the north Pacific in a small sailboat. I thought the ocean more dangerous and I had survived that, includ-ing two capsizes. Yet a flaw had crept into my reasoning, that shred of comfort that I so needed. All it required was a sudden snap of a tent pole to pierce the side of the tent and our little haven would be exposed to the gripping torrent, unleashing chaos everywhere. Surely it would be as devastating as being overwhelmed by moun-tainous waves in a storm at sea. Our Gortex bivvy sacs became a life raft, and I stuffed them with all the ingredients necessary for survival.

Lying for hours on end, with all tiredness satisfied, the mind was set free to wander through the past and drift off to examine the shape of the future. The wind played an orchestral accompaniment, sweeping along with majestic grace, influencing thoughts almost

On our 40th day on Kanchenjunga, in marginal weather, we move back to Camp 3 once more. (Photo Chris Chandler)

imperceptibly. The high times and the low. Struck by a sudden blast of unleashed energy, I found my inner soul exposed and vulnerable to the wind's force. Relentlessly, it bashed down on me without mercy, then when almost all hope was vanquished it would stop abruptly, only to laugh at my petty human weaknesses. The dragons of my mind had come out to play. We never played cards or read books for that would be too much of a distraction, an intrusion in this thinking process. Sometimes we would talk and share our thoughts.

It was during these stormbound days on the side of Kanchenjunga that the idea of an innovative medical clinic and education centre was born. We were both shocked by the condition of the schoolhouse in Pele. The wind had blown snow through the wide cracks in the walls and it had collected in drifts in the corners. The floor was frozen dirt. The only clue that it was a schoolroom was a blackboard on one wall and a collection of noisy, dirty little children with apple red cheeks and runny noses. Surely we could raise enough money at least to provide a warm building for the kids to learn the basic rudiments. Chris commented on the dedication of the government-employed schoolteacher who, far from his native village, was not dressed in the traditional clothes of the local mountain people, but in those of a hillsman. He was freezing cold, yet never asked a thing for himself, only to have some worm medicine for his needy children. We gave him a good supply but realised what a short-term answer it was. To make an effective intervention, the whole village needed an active preventive medicine programme. Part of the school building could be used for adult education projects. It was here that the human waste-composting ideas could be incorporated, along with other ideas such as hothouses to grow much needed vegetables and fruit.

Whilst we enthusiastically threw ideas back and forth, Mongol lay silently, encased in his own world. We would often try to draw him out of his shell by asking him what he thought and why. 'What did you dream about last night Mongol? Do you ever have interesting dreams? Why are you doing this insane thing with us?

The anticipated break in weather comes at the base of the rock band. Equipped with a bivouac sack and stove we are finally covering new ground. (Photo Chris Chandler)

What are you getting out of it?' Whether it was lack of understanding or just a reluctance to share his thoughts with two foreigners, he remained inscrutable. Even though we tried to include him in our discussions he was simply 'there' as an unobtrusive presence.

The difficult conditions of everyday life were taken as commonplace. Chris went outside to attend a call of nature. Hit by a blast of wind that knocked him off balance, it caused him to roll over in the unsavoury pile. His one-piece down suit was a mess. Chris's response to the whole incident, 'Well, that's the last shit I'm ever going to take,' made me fall over in paroxysms of laughter. Everything cleaned up quite easily as it froze solid. Our sense of smell had long been lost due to the effects of altitude.

In the early hours of 10 January, the wind gusts seemed to be losing some strength, and hit with less frequency. It was our 40th day on the mountain. Vain hopes already lain to rest began to reawaken. In anticipation we began the brews and studied the upper mountain and sky for other encouraging signs of a break in the weather.

Listening more to our instincts than to the scant evidence of weather improvement, we decided to move on up to Camp 3 and wait there for a more decisive change. We knew from previous experience just how quickly we could retreat should the weather turn for the worst. This time we took the tent. It was a slow start, stymied by indecision about the weather and breaking camp. We didn't want to be carrying an extra 20 kg (40 lb) of ice that had glued itself to the tent fabric. The pickets holding the tent in place had welded themselves to the ice and resisted extraction until the last moment. It all took time and patience and to complicate everything, the wind was still gusting strongly.

It was well after 10 am before we got moving. The wind, playing tricks, decided to increase in intensity. I was racked with doubts as to the wisdom of our decision. Only the thought that the five hours it took us to get ready would be wasted kept me from turning back. With each blast, forward movement was halted, not only because of the sheer force of the wind but due to the extreme breathlessness it caused in us.

As we drew closer to the ice gully that led to the first snow terrace, the feeling of doubt changed to dread. Something was wrong but I couldn't figure out what it was. Finally I realised a snow avalanche from above had poured over the rappel line we had left in place. The weight of the snow had torn the anchor loose and left the rope hanging down, with the loop used to attach to the anchor intact. Chris caught up with me. 'It looks just like a hangman's noose doesn't it?' I said, 'it gives me the creeps.' We warmed up our hands, Chris gave me an icy kiss and we started climbing upwards.

It was just before dark by the time we had dug a platform large enough for the tent to fit on, at least partially. We were about 60 m (200 ft) below the rock band. Erecting the tent in darkness with its complicated poles was an awful job. A sudden gust of wind sent a pole screaming off down the slope before we could do anything about it. My heart sank, the tent was useless without it and we had no spares.

Without warning, Chris took off into the darkness, and about 15 minutes later returned, pole in hand. I considered that finding the pole was a small miracle. We quickly slipped the runaway into place and the tent was erected. As soon as it was up we were hit with another tremendous blast threatening to carry all three of us into Tibet, still clinging to the tent. The struggle to keep in contact with the ground resulted in a large tear in the fly and tent itself. It was unfortunate, but we considered ourselves lucky to have a tent at all and hurriedly finished the task by securing the entire structure to the slope with our climbing rope, in a criss-cross fashion. Cold and tired, we climbed in, grateful to have some shelter from the wind.

Twenty-four hours passed. There seemed to be little change in the weather and we faced another long night of being battered. A large snowdrift was slowly overtaking the tent, sifting steadily through the tear which was on my side. To compound the problem, the zipper on the tent door gave its last gasp and broke. Everything was covered in snow and either wet or icy, including my sleeping bag. Chris's bag was no better. There was as much ice on the inside of my Gortex bivvy sac as on the outside. I couldn't believe how Mongol managed to keep his bag so dry, yet as he never moved except to eat the food I handed him, I guessed it really wasn't too much of a mystery. His bladder capacity was awesome.

In order to get enough heat from our stove to melt snow, a second stove was necessary to heat the gas cartridge of the first. Why was it nothing seemed to work the way it was supposed to when one's need was greatest? We had to get out of this awful place, either by going up or down.

By morning the weather looked a little improved, and with another woefully late start we moved on up to look at the rock band. It was now new territory and Chris and I were both excited and filled with anticipation. By the time we had reached the bergschrund and crossed over it, there was a feeling that it was quite late. Nonetheless curiosity pulled us onwards.

As this was the most technically demanding section of the face it was understood that Chris would do the leading, carrying his personal gear, camera and the hardware it was anticipated would be needed for the pitch. I would belay him, then Mongol and I would follow on up, carrying the rest of the equipment, either moving together or jumaring up the steeper sections. Due to the zig-zag nature of the route, however, it was hardly practical and we found it was necessary to climb most of the pitch anyway, passing the ice hammer back and forth between the two of us. As we only had one 45 m (150 ft) section of rope, there was a considerable amount of drag. Climbing with two ropes would have made the job easier but one had been sacrificed to save on weight. A mass of ropes led off in every direction imaginable — an ugly relic of past expeditions in such a pristine environment. Except for a few feet here and there, they were frozen and buried deep in the ice which made them largely unusable. Chris did manage, however, to take advantage of a few solid-looking anchors.

As we moved upwards, we left a series of our own ice screws behind for a quick and easy descent. The series of steep ice traverses and short rock overhangs made climbing difficult and strenuous, even as a second climber. It was definitely the hardest climb I had done so far in the Himalayas. We were about halfway up when it became obvious that we should either turn around or risk climbing into the night. As the weather seemed to be settling and Chris and I were both in good spirits, we decided to continue on. It was exhilarating to be making progress over new ground that for so many weeks had been unattainable. Big daddy wind had gone to sleep for a while. Chris's long-range weather forecast showed signs of coming true.

It was just before dusk and I had traversed about 4.5 m (15 ft) of steep hard ice which angled up, leading to a short, very steep, ice and rock gully that turned into a short, off-width, overhanging crack formed by large boulders either side. After making several passes I finally overcame the obstacles and hauled myself over the top. It was extraordinarily strenuous and I hoped there wouldn't be too many more surprises like that ahead. After an inexplicable delay of 10–15 minutes, when Mongol seemed to be fiddling around with equipment, he followed on up. I couldn't believe he had waited until it was his turn before deciding to do this. Didn't he realise how critical time was?

He began traversing across the ice, slipped a short distance, but was able to halt the fall. Up to this point, although slow, Mongol seemed to be taking the difficult climbing in his stride. Now he was showing signs of fatigue and I began to feel concerned. He completed the traverse and started on up the gully. He slipped again, the rope held him but he landed sideways. To our horror he rolled upside down, hanging limply on the end of the rope. 'Help! Pull me up.' 'You're going to have to climb up this rock yourself,' Chris shouted back. It was the beginning of a horror movie I had no desire to sit through.

As he lay upside down, moaning, Chris lowered down the loose end of the rope. 'You're going to be in big trouble if you let that pack fall off, it's got your sleeping bag in it, remember? Now grab this rope I'm lowering down to you and use it to pull yourself back upright.' 'I can't.' 'You've got no choice!' I started getting images of a frozen corpse on the end of our rope. I couldn't let it happen. I intervened with a different approach, 'Come on Mongol. Look, if I climbed up I know you can do it.' If the harsh and firm approach didn't work, I would try the soft maternal treatment. He started to move his arms around searching for the rope. I guided him to it.

Finally he grasped hold of it and in a few moves was upright again. 'My pack is too heavy, take it up.' 'You're carrying the same as Cherie, Chris replied.' This wasn't true but his was no more than 5 kg (10 lb) heavier. Chris continued, 'Besides, if we try to haul it, it will only get stuck. You're going to have to climb up with the

pack on. Now remember, have one try and make sure you get up.'
We both held our breath and in a few minutes he was with us.

It was now totally dark. Although it was only a few more pitches
to the top of the rock band, we were uncertain of the degree of
difficulty and thought it unwise to continue, tired and in the darkness. The dangerous incident with Mongol had put a dampener on
our spirits and cost us precious time.

There was only one platform which was reasonably flat and long
enough to lie down on. Chris told Mongol to take this place.
We would sit on a small ledge less than 25 cm (10 in) deep at the
top which sloped downwards and outwards to 75 cm (30 in) deep at
the bottom before it stopped abruptly. We had the choice of standing up all night, or trying to slip into our sleeping bags and sacs and
spend the night sitting down without sliding off the ledge. We
chose the sitting down method and tied off to a piton as a safeguard.

In return for the relative comfort Mongol was enjoying, the
trade-off was that he would make brews for everyone. He gave up
after a short while, complaining that he couldn't get the stove lit
and he was too cold anyway. We watched enviously as he arranged
his sleeping mat and bag, pulled the cover over his head and
disappeared into what appeared, at least in our eyes, to be the most
exquisite luxury imaginable.

I could feel Chris's resentment towards Mongol rise, along with
mine. However, I found myself intervening in the role of mediator,
always sensitive to mounting tension and eager to avoid it. I needed
to diffuse the situation. 'Well, we invited him to come along.
Besides, you know how weak the flame was even inside the tent at
Camp 3.' It made me feel better, at least, but I couldn't help
thinking Mongol could have tried a bit harder. 'Well,' I added, 'It
all makes for a good book, *Memories of My Most Memorable Nights
With My Lover.*' We both laughed and settled down to search for
what little comfort our tiny hold on the edge of the world could
provide.

Mongol's apparent lack of drive was a deepening concern, and I
cursed Bharat's influence on his decision to stay with us. This was
not the place to be merely to earn a salary or because someone 'told'
you to. Mongol had such a quiet, gentle nature. Over the months

of close living I had developed a deep affection for him, and with that came a tremendous sense of responsibility for his welfare. This was no tiger but a lamb.

The wind picked up and we began to get blasted with particles of ice sweeping down from the ice cliffs above. It was a hard way to take a shower, I thought, as particles came filtering into my bivvy sac and worked devious pathways down the back of my neck. I shuddered with the shock of cold. To make things worse, I kept sliding down the ledge and then had to worm my way back to the high point again. I wanted to avoid the risk of falling off and hanging free, for although I was tied into the rock above, the scenario of climbing back to my perch encased in a sleeping bag and bivvy sac did not appeal. All this wriggling around caused my sleeping bag to fall down to my knees inside the bivvy sac, and I never seemed to get it much higher than my waist. The down loft had sunk to the thickness of a pancake. Chris didn't appear to be much better off. He was sharing the wider part of the ledge along with my legs.

I kept a rotating selection of gloves drying inside my down suit. My hands were cold but 'under control', whereas my feet had long ago frozen. We had kept on our boots and crampons as it was too cramped even to contemplate removing them.

I desperately needed to empty my bladder. Having cut a large slit in the layers of long underwear at the beginning of the trip, I usually managed the procedure without difficulty. It was just a matter of undoing two zippers. Now, I was faced with the additional chore of safely securing my down bag and sac to prevent them from being blown away. Chris offered to take care of the problem. It was then necessary to remove my harness. I had to be careful, otherwise I could end up on the glacier 300 m (1,000 ft) below. Then I had to take off my wind jacket as the zipper to my down suit had frozen solid and I needed to loosen it. Following that I had to deal with wind pants that did not have a convenient zipper. In the struggle, a gust of wind blew away my wind parka. I wondered why I had bothered when I ended up peeing down my leg anyway. The loss of the wind parka was a serious mishap and I scolded myself rather lamely for letting it happen. But I didn't seem to be much colder without it. I wasn't shuddering and shaking, although the cold was undoubtedly 'present'.

Dawn came. We were covered in spindrift and dripping in icicles, 'Hey, this would make a great photo!' I commented enthusiastically. Chris was already up and moving around and I waited in expectation for him to record the moment, since he usually took most of the photos on the trip — unless I felt particularly inspired. The trouble was, if I got up to get the camera the subject would be gone from the photo, namely, 'Climber survives awful night on narrow rock ledge'. Somehow, taking a shot of the empty ledge where we had sat didn't quite capture it.

I was reminded of a photo I saw once in a book of claimed 'sightings' of the legendary Big Foot, who shares a similar heritage to the Yeti. It was a photo of a fence with a man standing beside it pointing. The caption read 'Fence where I saw Big Foot jump over'! I was disappointed when the photo didn't happen. It was probably too cold even to think about a photo, I reasoned, and started to move stiffly into action.

The remaining three pitches posed no difficulty and we set up the tent at the top of the rock band. Although it was still early in the morning we were cold and tired after the bivouac, and more than anything needed to rehydrate our bodies. The first cups of fluid I drank I vomited back up. Gradually we all started to feel better as we spent the entire day melting snow and drinking fluids.

The conditions inside the torn and battered tent were awful as we had done a poor job making the tent platform. There didn't seem to be a single flat spot anywhere and consequently as much fluid was spilt as was drunk. Chris was still angry at Mongol for his performance on the rock band, and insisted he do most of the cooking. I couldn't have agreed more, but the tension made me feel uncomfortable.

The condition of Chris's and my sleeping bags made them a pathetic help in providing warmth. Compacted and coated in ice, they were twice their normal weight. As mine seemed to be in the worst shape I decided to leave it behind for the summit bid, rather than carry the useless thing. Chris thought for a while, then decided to do the same.

The sky was marred intermittently with patches of dark cloud, the jetstream was held tenuously in suspension. We waited until dawn on 14 January which looked like a day full of promise. Perhaps we could do it in a single push. 'It was getting to be a habit, these late starts,' I thought to myself as we roped up. Breakfast alone had taken a record-breaking five hours. Still, who knew when we would have our next drink?

A small rock and ice gully marked the transition between the rock band and the second snow terrace. Smaller than the first snow terrace, it reached across in an expansive stretch of gentle 20–45 degree slopes, to terminate in several more steeper bands of rock and snow — our pathway to the summit. The Czechs had described how awful this section had been for them, of boring and exhausting work in thigh-deep snow. Our crampons scarcely marked the surface, much of which was bare ice.

We moved, roped together but without belays. This was no time for slipping and so we placed Mongol in the middle in the hope that if he did lose his footing, quick and simultaneous action by both Chris and me would hopefully prevent us all from being dragged to our deaths. The exposure was exciting; we were climbing only several hundred feet above towering ice cliffs that until now had always held us in subservience. 'Can you see us Lori, Bharat, Tirthay, Mingma? We made it this far, keep praying for us. We need your prayers.'

Yalung Kang's imposing north face dominated our view. It had a way of wanting to crowd us off the mountain. 'There is no room for you here,' it was saying. Like the uninvited wedding guest, we tried to act invisible and slide in through the side door. Our progress was encouragingly steady, although slow. The rock bands above were acting as a magnetic attraction, pulling me forward.

After what appeared an eternity we crossed over a bergschrund and started angling our way through a rock and snow couloir. The snow had collected in drifts between the rocks and for the first time it was necessary to plug steps. Chris continued leading and his momentum was staggering. I looked on in awe of his unflagging strength, feeling mine fading with every footstep. We exited the couloir to complete a long traverse under the final band of rock. We then turned and started to climb directly upwards. I called out to Chris, 'What's happening with my eyes, it's getting light and dark and light again. I think I'm going blind.' He called back, 'It's just the weather and clouds, for a moment I thought the same thing was happening to me.'

My love for Chris flowed freely. This was what we were meant to be doing. I tuned into his energy flow but I was incapable of matching it. I needed to stop and rest for a while. I called out to take a break and make brew. 'Look Cherie, it's so close, why don't I just slow down the pace.' We continued for about another 30 minutes. The intermittent dark periods had now changed to darkness, I realised. Chris was planning on climbing on through the night. I needed desperately to stop and make a brew. The weather was holding up, there was no wind, it was just me who was running out of steam. 'If we don't stop now I'm going to drop dead.' It was rather a dramatic announcement, but I just did not feel strong enough to climb on without a warm drink. It got the desired result.

Excerpt from Lori's diary: 'Early afternoon we see them establishing Camp 5. I have never seen anything like this action. It's incredibly exciting. Weather getting terribly grim up there. Increase in heavy fog (dark) rolling in. I see them milling around most likely looking for a camping spot (— 1.30 pm). I wonder if it hadn't been for the change in weather they would have continued on. I'm sure they are pushing it to the limit.'

We looked around for a place to stop. 'How about up by that rock.' It was 15 m (50 ft) away. 'Too far. There's plenty of snow here. This will do.' We started to dig a shelter. The result was a crescent-shaped tunnel with two entrances. It was long enough for us all to lie down in, would protect us from the wind, provide plenty of ventilation and there was no danger of us falling down the slope. Satisfied, we threaded our way into it. Here we would rest, make brews, see what was happening with the weather and wait until dawn to make the final summit push. Only 600 m (2,000 ft) of climbing remained. It looked like we had it in the bag.

9

Do not stand at my grave and weep.
I am not there, I do not sleep.
I am a thousand winds that blow,
I am the diamond glint on snow.

ANONYMOUS

WE ESTIMATED our snow cave to be close to 7,800 m (26,000 ft). As Chris occupied the flattest part of it and the door was in front of him providing good ventilation, he got the job of melting fluids for everyone. I was so tired I felt sick but managed to keep the liquid down without vomiting. We ended up having about two cups each, I think, as several got spilt. We snuggled up against each other. I was lying beside Chris's legs, and Mongol beside my legs. Mongol's feet stuck out of the other entrance to the cave. It was pretty cramped and very cold, but gradually we settled down.

I had one down mitt but couldn't find the other, it had got lost somewhere in the shuffle. The cold was really deep inside me and occasionally I would shudder, but manage to control it. Then one of us would feel stiff or get a cramp and we'd all have to move together to find a slightly different position. Chris, being the biggest, had a hard time getting comfortable and thrashed his legs about a few times.

It is hard to describe what it's like, that world up there, so cold that you barely feel anything. Your brain is so starved of oxygen that it floats freely, drifting in and out of a dream world. Yet there is a fragile thread that holds you and what you are doing to this world. We were where we wanted to be. Somewhere, deep down inside, I recognised a feeling of excitement that we were going for the summit in a few hours. We had waited so long for it.

Morning came, Chris stuck his head out the door and announced the weather was still good. He started melting snow for more brews. We hadn't had enough to drink the night before and it seemed important to get at least three cups each. With a few spills, I remember having only one cup before I needed to get up and move around. I felt incredibly stiff and could barely move my arms and legs. I put my crampons on inside the cave while Chris tended the stoves.

It usually took forever threading the straps and tightening them up with bulky mittens, but I had a system that worked using the tip of my ice axe to perform any fine manipulation. This morning I managed the procedure quite smoothly. Feeling pleased, I climbed outside to check on the weather myself. When I got up I discovered the missing down glove. I was disappointed to find it had frozen solid to the ground underneath my body. It was useless, I couldn't even get my hand into it. I still had my woollen gloves, polypro-polyn mitts and the heavy woollen mitts in use. Three pairs of woollen gloves in the pack remained as extras.

Outside, the weather still looked good and I stood gazing up at the summit and the route we would take to get there. I looked over at Chris to see what he was doing and with horror realised that the flames on both stoves had blown out. Chris was sitting inside the cave breathing in raw gas fumes without noticing what had happened. I flipped out, asking him what he thought he was doing. He just smiled happily back at me, almost as if he was drunk. I dragged him outside and sat him down. 'Take deep breaths. You need fresh air in your lungs. Come on sweetheart, breathe deep for me. Please.'

Whatever I said made no difference. All he wanted to do was go back and lie down. I couldn't stop him. 'Come and lie down with me sweetie. I just need to lie down for a while.' I crawled in and lay beside him. He put his arms around me affectionately. 'Yeah, I feel better now, much better.' It felt good for me too but I became restless, I just couldn't lie there for long. 'I have to get up and move around. You still need to put on your crampons. I'll wait for you outside.'

I wanted to check on Mongol. He had taken a considerable time to put on his crampons and harness and now sat staring up at the summit, apparently ready to go. That was good. I turned back to discover Chris staring at his feet. It was obvious to me that he was trying but was unable to fit the crampons by himself. I didn't like what had just happened, but this really confirmed my fears.

It was at this stage that I decided to descend. Chris then turned to me and said he didn't feel well, felt as though he had pneumonia. His chest started to gurgle. He began to gag, bringing up thick, green, foul-looking sputum. It was strange to see him gag, his white lips pursed and his face deep purple. It seemed he was getting bad fast. Even he realised it and agreed with my decision to descend. 'Yeah, it's time for us to go down, at least to 24,000 feet,' he said.

I started trying to put on his crampons but he wasn't holding still and it was really awkward. I was working away in my woollen mitts, wool gloves and polypropolyn liners when he said, 'I can't see anything, I'm blind.' My heart froze and at the same time my fingers turned stiff and claw-like. My body must have got a sudden rush of adrenalin and clamped down the blood vessels to the extremities, the result of surging fear. It was only now I realised that Chris had probably developed cerebral oedema, and I had been blaming the fumes from the stove on his deteriorating condition.

Time became even more critical and I tore off the gloves to look at my hands. The fingers had become white and marble-like. I knocked them together. It sounded as though I was banging two pieces of wood against one another. 'Look at my hands.' I showed them to Chris. He giggled, 'They are pretty bad, aren't they?' I left the gloves off, for in order to do any manipulation at all, the claws needed to be exposed. Periodically I would pull the sleeves of my jacket over them to try and warm them up a bit, and then continue working. Both hands had lost all feeling at this stage and I began imagining them being cut off at the wrist. 'Can't worry about that now. Got to concentrate on saving the whole body. That's what's important now. Got to save the body.'

Finally Chris's crampons were on. I had to get his harness on next, but he couldn't stand up without toppling over. I was beginning to lose my vision, too. It was like peering through a foggy car window on a rainy night. I became even more anxious, fearing that soon I would also succumb. I screamed out to Mongol to help.

'What the hell have you been doing all this time anyway?' He acted surprised that we were going down.

Supported between the two of us, we finally got the harness in place and Chris was tied into the rope. As he couldn't walk without falling over, I put Mongol and Chris together on the rope, moving down on a fixed belay. Chris leant on Mongol so heavily at times that they would both fall down, but were held tight by the rope. Slowly we made progress downwards. We were now traversing under the top band of rock.

Chris started to topple over and Mongol couldn't support him. I fell onto the ice axe but was yanked off and followed them falling down the slope. We must have dropped about 90–120 m (300–400 ft) before the rope snagged on a frozen snowdrift. I was surprised we'd fallen so far, and that we'd stopped about 9 m (30 ft) before a cliff. If the rope hadn't snagged we would have travelled over the edge. Well, that's one way of getting down the mountain, I thought to myself.

Packs and various pieces of equipment were scattered over the slope. Mongol unroped and collected it all. Chris was shaken up, but it woke him up a bit more and he started moving better by himself. I looked at the large hole in my glove liner caused by the passage of the rope. I hadn't been able to grasp hold of the rope and it had just passed through my hand.

The fall caused us to lose a little too much altitude and so we had to climb back up about 30 m (100 ft) before descending by the correct route. Now I placed Chris in the middle of the rope, trying to take advantage of both Mongol's and my belay should he fall again. He moved tenuously between us, stumbling and falling but being held in check by the tight rope.

We had just finished coming through the couloir of the top rock band and were standing resting. It was getting dark already, I couldn't believe it had taken so long to cover such a short distance. Where had the time gone? Still, at least we had made it so far, safe and sound. I turned around and saw Chris untie himself. 'What are you doing? Please don't!' 'I was just trying to help, he replied.' I tied him back in again while he stood meekly, looking like a scolded child.

I turned to discuss with Mongol what our plans should be. Chris

had untied himself again. He was playing a game with us! I recognised a cheeky grin on his face. Oh! God please help us. Mongol
saw my hands as I was tying Chris back into the rope. 'You stupid,
stupid girl. Put gloves on!' I had tried to but at this stage they were
so swollen and stiff, even the mitts wouldn't fit. I continued to pull
my sleeves down to cover the hands, which helped a little.

Mongol led off as I moved along with Chris. I couldn't take my
eyes off him for a minute. We staggered along like a couple of
drunks coming home from a New Year's Eve party, and shared a
joke about what bad shape we were in. I had wanted to make it
down about another 90 m (300 ft) to a bergschrund which I remembered on the way up. It looked as though it would provide a good
bivvy site, but in the dark and feeling completely exhausted, with
Chris likely to fall at any moment, it seemed wiser to stop where
we were, just below the rocks, on a gentle snow slope. Mongol
dug out a platform and we got ready to put Chris in his bivvy sac.

I asked Mongol to give Chris his sleeping bag, as he was a dying
man and badly needed it. I thought it might just make the difference and tip the scales in favour of life. Mongol refused to part with
it. A feeling of rage overwhelmed me. But how could I demand
that Mongol give it up? It was, after all, our choice to leave the
bags behind. The rage dissipated into a feeling of despair. I lay
beside Chris to try to warm him up. He showed me that one of his
hands was swollen and blue-looking. He must have lost a glove
when we fell. 'Put it under your arm sweetheart, try and warm it
up.' Mongol was digging another platform and I asked him to melt
snow instead, as Chris desperately needed a hot drink. After being
initially restless, Chris had settled down. He was still saying a few
words to me.

I needed to empty my bladder and stood up to do so but I
couldn't get the harness undone, or undo the zipper. I was becoming distraught. Chris looked up at me and said, 'Just pee down your
leg. It doesn't matter. I did.' His voice was kind and reassured me
that really everything was going to be OK after all. I let the muscles
go, and felt the warmth flow down my leg and fill my boots. I was
horrified to see surface the raw and basic instinct for survival.
Where lay the separation between us and animals, after all? I shuddered, retracting from the thought.

We had tied Chris off to an ice axe to prevent him sliding down the slope, but I wanted to use another ice axe as a back-up to the first. Chris was lying on part of the rope and my bivvy sac. I needed to get at both. I gently started easing the bag from under him. Trying to help me he suddenly lurched over to one side. In the process he slid off the ledge. I pulled him back into place but he was now restless again, tossing himself around on the narrow platform. I couldn't control him, I needed help. I called to Mongol.

Chris slid off the platform again. Mongol began complaining that I'd already told him to melt snow, now I was telling him to help Chris, and why didn't I make up my mind etc. etc. I was putting all my weight on the ice axe for fear it would be pulled out as Chris was now standing up in the bivvy sac, fearing he was in danger. He panicked and tried to run, but of course got caught up in the bag. His last words were, 'Will somebody help me?' and then he fell down on the snow. He must have exerted an enormous amount of energy in those final moments.

Mongol had been standing motionless, watching the whole scene. He now came over and helped me lower Chris to the partially built platform where he had been standing before. My rage at Mongol overwhelmed me again. Then I saw Chris's limp hand fall out of the bivvy sac. It was mottled and deep blue. We turned him over to look at his face.

His finely sculptured features, gaunt from weeks of gruelling work, had relaxed into an expression of bliss. All the tension and cares of mortal beings had dissolved, there was only peace and beauty shining forth. His skin was warm and glowed with colour. I bent down to kiss his lips. They were strangely lifeless. I couldn't feel his breath upon my cheeks, only perfect stillness.

As death and love met, my whole being filled with terror, I felt him letting go of the past and all that we had shared, yet the future had not arrived. I couldn't let him go so easily, 'I need you Chris, don't leave me!' I screamed in silence.

I searched for a pulse in his neck, but with frozen fingers it was futile. I should have realised there would be no sensation. I showed Mongol where to feel but his hands were also too cold. I started doing mouth to mouth resuscitation, but the awkward angle of the snow slope made holding Chris's head in the necessary position too heavy for me to handle. I couldn't get a proper seal, and air wasn't passing into his lungs. Sobbing with frustration I tried to open the zipper to the bivvy sac. It was frozen solid, coated in ice.

Mongol tried but was unable to open it either. I went through the motions of chest compressions and blowing into his mouth. It was only a few cycles before I fell down exhausted. The cold sank its teeth into me. I pressed my body against Chris's to feel his warmth and love. The sounds of Mongol's wailing and moaning penetrated my mind. He shared my sense of abandonment and loss. We were being swallowed up by the immense black void of the night. I cared little for Mongol's agony, there was nothing we could do to yell or wail our way out of it. Chris had started on another journey.

I realised Mongol had gone to his sleeping bag. As I lay there looking into a bottomless pit, I was drawn closer and closer to the edge. I was suspended in space, I wanted to go with Chris, to seek out where he had gone. A subtle presence became more strongly felt. I recognised it as my two children standing there beside me, looking solemnly at the scene without pleading, grief or tears. I sensed their need for guidance and counsel, especially over the next few years. Although they never asked for help I turned towards them, and Chris went on alone.

Now I could feel myself being sucked into a vacuous space. Overcome with terror I clawed my way back out of it. I couldn't lose my grip even for one moment, and lying there beside Chris I was being drawn into that tunnel, towards the journey I had turned my back on. I was being overpowered.

I got up and moved about 3 m (10 ft) up to a higher platform and crawled into my bivvy sac. I lay motionless, looking up into the immensity of the night sky. Never had its presence been so vast and all pervasive. Away from Chris I felt safer and in the bivvy sac, warmer too. Time stood still. I heard Chris's familiar cough, but instead of coming from below where he lay, it was coming from above, a few feet to the left of me, close to where Mongol lay.

I expected Mongol to jump up and run away in fright but he didn't move a muscle. Then Chris's voice called out my name; it sounded urgent, as though he wanted my attention. It startled me and I sat up. Why didn't Mongol seem to hear it? He was probably too terrified. I looked around. Chris's body was motionless. I soon realised, from the echoing quality of the voice, that it had come from the tunnel. I lay down again, more afraid of losing my mind with grief than dying from cold.

I lay there examining the fine tapestry that life weaves, looking at the design that brought Chris and my coloured threads together, to blend into the overall pattern. I marvelled at the way the individual stitches fit together so neatly to create such a thing of beauty. I focused on one stitch. It was a scene in San Francisco, after work in the intensive care unit. Lori was telling me about a dream she had: 'There are three people on the mountain, one person is sitting by himself underneath some rocks while the other two are climbing down alone.'

My heart started to pound in my chest. Relentlessly the film rolled on, projecting the images on the screen. 'There will be much falling.' We'd already done that, but I should be careful. I remembered the lost glove, I slept on it all night. You're right Lori, I should have been more careful about my hands. Like a soothing balm, I was no longer afraid, I was enveloped in calm and peace. The movie rolled on. 'Well, do we live or do we die?' 'That won't be known till the very last moment.'

Morning came. I had great difficulty in bending my arms and legs. The pernicious cold was taking a stronger grip. Mongol and I went down to Chris. I pulled back the cover and looked inside. His face was grey, drained of life. His mouth hung open. Purple lips defied me. I shrank back, recoiling in horror, and Mongol started making strange wailing noises. I lay down to embrace his body. The sounds that came from within were empty and hollow. Lost, I didn't know what to do. The traditional climber's burial, by placing the body in a crevasse, repulsed me. Pushing the body over a cliff was equally disgusting. No. He would sit where he was, in dignity, with his pack and ice axe beside him, gazing out over the vast Tibetan plateau.

I saw his watch and for some reason felt it was important to take it with me. The struggle to get it off his frozen hand made me feel disgusted for even trying. I remembered a small tape recorder tucked inside his down suit. What a beautiful record to have of our trip, yet I knew, from the night before, we couldn't get the zipper open. I wanted to place photos of my children on his body as a token of their love for him, to help him on his journey, but I couldn't part with them. I needed them for myself, for my own journey back to the world of the living. I felt reassured by the fact that he kept photos of his own kids tucked safely next to his heart. We had planned to place the photos of our children on the summit. This was a summit of a different kind.

I said goodbye to Chris and now it was time to go. I realised Mongol was still wailing loudly. 'One die, now we all die,' he was carrying on in a distracted manner. I groaned inside when I realised he had no intention of going down the mountain with me. I told him I wasn't going to wait around and die, I had two children waiting for me. He had loved ones too, I reminded him, who were awaiting his return. It just sent him off again on another long series of moans and crying.

I don't remember how long all this took, but I was getting quite impatient. I tied him into the rope and started climbing down. The rope soon became taut because Mongol was refusing to take a single footstep. I had to lean with all my weight against the rope. One step forward and he would stop again. I'd pull again with all my might, and he would take another hesitant step. It occurred to me we must have looked a funny pair. I felt like a yak herder dealing with an unruly yak. The slope was gentle, so I didn't have to worry too much about losing my footing and could be quite aggressive. Gradually the tension eased off and I felt Mongol following on behind. Every so often he would stop moving and start wailing. I'd give the rope a strong pull and he would start advancing again. Every now and then he would stall completely, only to start again. It gave me strength and comfort to feel Chris's presence watching on.

We were now moving over bare ice and the angle of the slope had steepened considerably. The slopes dropped off in vertical cliffs a short distance below. It occurred to me that I should be placing ice screws for protection against a possible fall since not only were my feet frozen and legs stiff and wooden-like, but we were both at the limit of exhaustion. Mongol had settled down and was moving along with me. I didn't want to lose the momentum we had gained by stopping, and possibly risk having him stall on these steeper slopes, never to start moving again, so we continued on. Gradually, the gully that led to our tent at the top of the rock band came into view. I started climbing down it, still facing outwards, then descended the vertical section facing towards the slope. My crampon slipped a fraction of an inch but I wasn't particularly worried. I thought I could halt the minor slip. Suddenly my body took off at great speed. 'Mongol, take care and stop me falling. I'm falling Mongol, aren't you going to stop me?' My head hit a rock. It was supposed to hurt — I'm sure it should have hurt. 'Well, it looks like we're taking the quick way down after all.'

Suddenly everything became still. I lay there for a while, stunned. I got up and looked round for Mongol. Was he OK? The rope had snagged behind a mound of ice. I had fallen on one side of it, Mongol had fallen on the other side. Once again we had stopped just before the vertical drop of the rock band. My mind and body had separated. I watched myself get up and start climbing mechanically, devoid of any feeling, towards the tent 30 m (100 ft) above. I wondered what power was moving my body, because it wasn't mine.

Mongol had unroped, and began traversing the ice mound to the tent. He looked unhurt. Leaving the rope in a frozen, tangled mess, we climbed in. Torn sides meant it was full of snowdrifts, so we had to clear aside a place to sit. But where was Chris? My heart began to sob, while I looked on without a sign of passion.

It was necessary to start the stove to melt fluids. I tried but my hands were useless. Mongol refused, complaining that his hands would also freeze. 'Light the stove.' I was surprised at the threatening tone of my voice. I still had not forgiven Mongol for his refusal to help Chris in his last moments. Actually, he did the best he could, but I failed to see it at the time. Taking heed of me now, he finally got the stove lit. I took over the job of melting snow and we both sucked on the warm fluid. I vomited up several cups, but finally the liquid settled in my stomach and I began to feel more restored, benefiting also from the lower elevation. This was to be the fourth day that jetstream winds had been held in check. How much longer could the weather hold? I climbed into my frozen sleeping bag, grateful for its psychological benefit, if nothing else.

Next morning we started off the first three rappels without

difficulty, although pulling down the ropes created a lot of drag. The effort made me realise just how weak I had become. Even climbing over easy ground, when the rope would catch and pull on something, Mongol had an annoying habit of pulling down on the rope, making it snag more firmly, instead of flicking the rope over the obstacle. He was still doing this after we finished a rappel and were ready to start on the next one. I had chosen to go first to make sure I located the ice screws and anchors we had left in place. I barely had the strength to pull the rope down, let alone climb back up to relieve the places where the rope had jammed. My annoyance at Mongol's persistent habit made me merciless in sending him back up to do the job. After all, wasn't it his carelessness that had caused the rope to snag? In actual fact, the zig-zag nature of the descent route would have made it a delicate problem for any climber.

I had the thought of rappelling straight down the rock face rather than following our ascent route, but I didn't like the look of several other rappel lines that dropped off eerily into the void below. I only had one rope and half a dozen extra ice screws and a few pitons. Besides, by the nature of the rock formations, the problem of snagging may not be solved even then. I didn't like the idea of wandering around on unknown ground that looked even steeper than what we were on already.

Mongol's lack of experience, combined with both our weak conditions, did not make for a quick and easy descent. It was approaching dark and we had just completed the final eight rappels. We had roped together and I was traversing the band of snow when there was another inexplicable delay. Had the rope snagged again? No answer. It was now dark. I thought he must have frozen in fright. I sat in the snow and waited, staring down at my claws. My anger towards Mongol was generated by a feeling of impotence, by not being able to do anything about the unfairness of what had happened, and what was happening now. Finally, I let the anger go, for what was there of any value to be lost. At last I saw him climbing slowly towards me. I thought the rope must have snag-ged, but I still didn't fully understand as it was easy ground and should have posed no problem.

Mongol removed his pack to look for a flashlight as the battery in mine was dead. To my horror, the pack rolled down the mountain containing his sleeping bag, bivvy sac and the stove. 'Looks like another day and night without drinking,' I thought grimly. Mongol was clearly shaken up about losing it. I saw this as an opportunity to demonstrate to Mongol the kind of behaviour I had expected from him towards Chris. I offered him the use of my sleeping bag. Without a moment's hesitation he accepted, and climbed in gratefully. 'Well, what's another night out to me anyway?' I thought lamely, even if the lesson had been lost on Mongol.

Mongol must have had a change of heart during the night. By morning he was saying we were going to die again. He refused to move from the sleeping bag. The impotence I had felt and lain to rest reawakened, manifesting itself once more in anger. 'I'll tell Cheney, I'll see to it you'll never get another job!' I failed to see what an idiotic thing I was saying — if he was dead, he'd hardly be in need of a job. Anyway, my ranting and raving made little difference, he had made up his mind to die.

Letting go of my self-righteousness diffused my anger, and compassion crept in. My yelling must have started to get him down. I felt bad that I had been treating him so harshly. I put my arms around him and held him closely. I could feel his body slowly charge with energy. I talked about the good progress we had made so far, how the worst was now behind us and we were going to make it back together. With new heart Mongol retrieved the rope and found his pack. After melting snow and drinking for four hours, we descended to the ice gully.

I was just about to start the first rappel when Mongol started to topple over backwards. I grabbed him just in time before he fell 120 m (400 ft) down a very steep ice gully. I told him to sit down and wait for me to finish rappelling. Finally we both stood at the bottom and began unroping and coiling line.

Mongol suddenly toppled over backwards again. Before I could grab him he was slipping and sliding another 90–120 m (300–400 ft). I followed along a trail of blood to discover a frostbitten nose had been scraped, but there were no other injuries apart from some bruises.

Chastened by the experience, we moved slowly down to our old Camp 2. Urine-stained snow was all that remained. Where was the joy and beauty that we had shared? It was just a memory. I looked up at the place where Chris sat and saw him looking down. His departure and its irrevocable nature had left me with a profound sense of loss. I thought back to the night he had died, heard him coughing and calling my name. Maybe he hadn't gone so far away after all?

We still had the lower icefall to descend. We had climbed down it without difficulty before, but this time was different — it presented yet another major hurdle to overcome. Lori's answer to my question kept ringing in my ears: 'Well, do we live or do we die?' 'That won't be known till the very last moment.' I now took it as a very strong warning and chose to spend the night at Camp 2, trying to rest and drink more fluids. Mongol refused to take any more after drinking only one cup, and I vomited up most of what I drank.

Night came, along with the long anticipated change in weather. The upper mountain was socked in once more and we were blasted by wind and driving snow. Kanchenjunga had given us a merciful reprieve but it was now time to get off. Yet there was still another night to endure, faced with the doubts in my mind. I was tormented by the thought that I may have been able to alter the course of events. Climbing back down the mountain, every time I passed a stain of blood-tinged sputum in the snow it tore my heart out. Most of it I believe was Chris's, although I too had been coughing up the stuff. Earlier in the trip we had talked about it coming from our nasal passages, but now I wondered if it hadn't also been coming from our lungs.

If only I could have shown how much more I loved him . . . been more accepting of his total being. I thought back to Seattle, to the day of our departure for Kathmandu. I saw how much Annamae and Howard, Chris's parents, loved their son so much. The last words I had said to them were, 'Don't worry, I'll bring him back alive.' How could I explain adequately all those choices we made that led ultimately to Chris's death. The incessant judging and self-doubt continued through the night.

In the morning Mongol wanted to leave the rope behind and I wanted to take it. We compromised by trying to cut it in half. Undaunted by the fact that we had weakened the rope considerably by chopping it unsuccessfully, we dragged the whole thing along anyway. We realised we were terribly weak and needed to discard everything that wasn't absolutely necessary. Removing harnesses, we tied the rope around our waists. Our hardware consisted of two ice screws. We had sleeping gear, the stove, one gas cartridge and a handful of raisins each. On reaching the first of the two ice gullies, I belayed Mongol down. I was barely able to grasp my ice axe and hammer with my frozen hands, and had I been thinking clearly would have rappelled. Instead I chose to down climb. 'Have you got a good belay, Mongol?' 'Yes Memsahib.'

I hadn't gone far before I fell. Mongol's belay proved to be solid and he held the fall after about 9 m (30 ft). My down suit was torn, a crampon had come off and my leg had been struck by a rock. I felt nothing. We rappelled down the second ice gully without incident. The remaining ice screw got us to the safety of the lower glacier and moraine, but not before Mongol fell once more, this time on gentle ice slopes as we moved along together. He was looking punch drunk, and I wondered how I appeared to him.

We now faced the long walk back to Base Camp. I moved a few feet before realising just how profoundly weak I was, too far gone to carry a pack. Mongol decided to jettison his pack too. We were going for broke and left everything behind. 'Remember, Cherie, whether you live or whether you die, it won't be known till the very last moment.' I was counting on our Base Camp crew moving into alert. Perhaps they had already started on their way up the

RIGHT: *Approaching the top of the first rock band at 7,200 m (24,000 ft). Our snail-like progress is watched intently through binoculars by our friends below at Base Camp. They are unable to help us in any way, except by prayer. (Photo Chris Chandler)*

OVERLEAF: *'By our calculations, thinking of nothing else, by our desires, abandoning every other hope, by our efforts, renouncing all bodily comfort, we gained entry into this new world. So it seemed to us. But we learned later that if we were able to approach Mount Analogue it was because the invisible doors of that invisible country had been opened for us by those who guard them. The cock crowing in the milky dawn thinks its call raises the sun; the child howling in a closed room thinks its cries cause the door to open. But the sun and the mother follow courses set by the laws of their own beings. Those who see us even though we cannot see them opened the door for us, answering our puerile calculations, our unsteady desires, and our awkward efforts with a generous welcome.'* (Mount Analogue, René Daumal) *(Photo Chris Chandler)*

moraine? Watching our progress with binoculars, they must have realised something was terribly wrong. I bet Lori was freaking out, with the memory of the dream.

I doubted very much if we could survive another night out, without shelter, food or drink. The temptation to lie down was overwhelming. I sank down into the soft comfort of a waterbed, but realised this was a danger sign since boulders weren't supposed to feel like waterbeds. I roused myself and slowly moved on.

My mind was agile, dancing about, eager to be set free from the worn out body that encased it. 'I was never so alive as when I was dying.' I had read these words somewhere, and now was experiencing what the writer meant. My life was laid out before me in sparkling clarity on the pathway of boulders that led to Pang Pema. It all made sense, even the deep pain that I carried with me. I was set free, I had found a small corner to rest and reflect where there was harmony and peace.

We were now approaching the old site of Camp 1. I was so thirsty that the desire for fluid drove me on. Wistfully I looked back to the warmer summer months and how the glacier was running, dripping with water. Now there were only icicles to break off and suck on, to moisten my lips a little. Sometimes I would greedily crunch into the ice and swallow it, causing my stomach to cramp. This was a dangerous practice, since it would cause me to lose even more body heat, but I could scarcely control the urge. Then I would force a few raisins down, coaxing my body to accept the energy it needed to survive.

We drew closer to Camp 1. I began to pick out a distant figure

ABOVE: *'And I, to save my soul again*
Would tramp to sunsets grand
With sad-eyed mates across the plain
In the Never-Never Land.'
(Henry Lawson) (Photo Chris Chandler)

BELOW: *'The precious pot containing my riches becomes my teacher in the very moment it breaks. This lesson on the inherent impermanence of all things is a great marvel.' (Milarepa) (Photo Lori Orlando)*

PREVIOUS PAGE: *The last photograph Chris took. This is on the second snow terrace at about 7,500 m (25,000 ft).*

sitting on a glacier. I stared hard. Yes, it was Mingma in shorts and crampons, of all things, sitting there with a giant teapot full of steaming hot tea. I laughed in joy and anticipation — here were we, numb with cold, and he's sitting there in shorts! I could feel how good that hot tea would be, sliding down my parched throat. I staggered on. I was curious to see Mongol's reaction to this gift of mercy. There was none. He continued walking, without even stopping to say hello. I choked back a sob. 'Be careful, Cherie, things are getting weird. I know a drink would have been nice but you'll get one eventually. Just keep putting one foot in front of the other and you'll get there.'

It was beginning to get dark. I hoped by now they had seen us arrive at Camp 1. I was starting to feel we weren't going to make it to Base Camp. I needed a drink so badly. Now it was totally dark. Mongol had gone on ahead and I could no longer see him. 'Well, good luck to him, there's no sense in waiting around for me.' I felt like a child lost in the forest with malevolent spirits lurking close by. I made my way timidly through the trees.

I could hear the sharp noise of an ice axe clanging on boulders. I saw a dark figure approaching. A tiny voice came from within, 'Is that you Mongol, did you come back to look for me?' 'Cherie, it's you ... then it must have been Chris.' Bharat put his arms around me.

Giant sobs, deep strange moans I had no control over, came pouring out in anguish and relief. 'Where's Mongol?' 'We found him sitting on a rock, staring at his headlamp. He couldn't talk at first but he's better now after drinking. Here's some tea, it's still warm. Take it slowly now, not so fast.'

It was 10.30 pm by the time we arrived at Base Camp. Dear Lori was poised, waiting, with large pots of warm water ready to thaw our frozen extremities. Like everyone else, she was surprised that it was me who had returned. 'Oh, Chris, poor sweet Chris!' Emotions kept in tight check, she began removing my urine-soaked clothing and boots. I could feel her pain as she examined our frozen hands and feet. Blood pressures were in the low 70s, pulses couldn't be felt. 'Well, I know you're alive,' she said. During the unthawing we expected pain but there was none. It took weeks to absorb the fact that the nerves had died long ago.

I dropped into a dreamless sleep, unaware that Lori and Mingma had given us their sleeping bags. They sat through the night, huddled by the kerosene heater, hugging each other to keep warm. I opened my eyes to daylight, sunshine and warmth. Through the tent door I could see the rolling slopes that led to Drohmo. Suddenly I recognised the silhouette of Chris's figure standing, watching. I sat up. It had all been a bad dream, just a nightmare to be forgotten. He was standing there the way he always did, looking up at the north face. I was crying I was so happy. He turned and walked towards the tent. Soon he would be with me again. The figure stopped and turned once more to look back at the mountain — it was only a goat.

Four days passed. Mingma was running the mountain trails to reach Tapeljung. He hoped to arrive there in seven days and send a telegram requesting a helicopter. The radio at the Ghunsa checkpost was out. On the way, he had left word about the tragedy with the people of Ghunsa. Now they arrived, gathering round in a mixture of curiosity and compassion. They had received the news in the middle of one of the more important religious feasts. Dropping everything immediately, half the village left to come to our assistance. The concern that Chris showed towards these people had made a lasting impression. This was an outpouring of love and sorrow for the departed soul of a man who had showed that he cared. Bharat was crying when he told me, 'They don't expect to be paid Cherie, they just want to help.' Mongol and I were loaded into straw baskets which were supported and balanced on the porters' headbands, and the journey down the narrow and often precipitous trail began. The helicopter would pick us up at Pele.

I bid my last farwell to Kanchenjunga and the place where Chris's body sat. I drifted off, looking up at the sky and surrounding peaks. The sky was heavily overcast with ominous-looking clouds travelling quickly past. I detected a bright gold outline that framed a large grey cloud. Finally the rays of sun came spilling through, creating a shaft of light which fell on my chest. A passageway was formed, leading to infinity.

Slowly I felt Chris's spirit, that had enveloped and protected me, gathering itself together. A giant vacuum was left as he departed. Tears flowed, but I knew it would be wrong to hold him back.

APPENDIX A

FROSTBITE

In the mountains the most severe (deep) frostbite is almost always the result of a 'live or die' situation, when the body is pumping full of adrenalin, the most potent blood vessel (vaso) constrictor known to man. The heavy breathing that accompanies fear and exertion increases loss of fluid through the lungs. There is often little opportunity to stop and make a hot drink which would help warm the body and combat the effects of dehydration.

The primary injury is thought to be the result of water — present not only in the cells that comprise of the blood vessels and tissue, but also surrounding the cells — forming ice crystals. When water turns into ice it loses volume, resulting in a loss of total blood volume. Collapsed cell walls fall onto the sharp corners of the ice crystals and are damaged more easily than a cell that is fully hydrated. In addition, the walls of the blood vessels themselves become friable and weakened and begin to leak. Capillaries just one cell thick are first to become clogged with ice crystals and debris. Larger blood vessels soon follow with oedema and general microscopic haemorrhaging. Oxygen is not carried to the tissues, or waste products taken away.

What can the climber do, assuming he is adequately clothed, to lessen the risk of permanent damage and subsequent amputation due to exposure to cold, i.e. to keep what might be superficial frostbite from converting to deep frostbite? Climbers should be cautioned strongly against the use of vasodilating drugs such as Dibenzaline and those derived from certain species of the Rauwolfia root. Their action is to block the effects of the sympathetic nervous system responsible for producing adrenalin. The result is an increased blood flow to the skin, mucosa and abdominal viscera. Accompanying the vasodilatory effect is a drop in blood pressure which may be profound and debilitating. This drop in blood pressure increases the body's fluid requirement to 4-8 litres (7-14 pints) per day. A slight to moderate dehydration may become critical, aggravating the frostbite even further and will also worsen the effects of chronic hypothermia.

Understanding that fear and anxiety produce an involuntary 'shut-down' of peripheral vessels is one way of recognising what is happening and stepping in to take control of these emotions. The Tibetan Yogis realised that by inducing a state of profound relaxation using visualisation techniques, 'warming oneself in the snows without fire' was possible. Scientists in the west have discovered that alpha waves are produced in the brain when one meditates. A person can be trained to alter brain activity and produce vasodilation naturally, by being hooked up to a 'bio-feedback' machine. This is not normally possible voluntarily. Thermostatic electrodes are placed on various parts of the skin and a hypnotic, trance-like state is induced. The 'feedback' is the screen that records temperature variation. It is interesting to observe that 'effort' produces a fall in temperature; one must practise 'letting go' for an *increase* in temperature to occur. The high hopes following discovery of bio-feedback in the 1960s and its proposed use in control of bodily functions and disease have largely been put aside. Regulating blood pressure levels and producing a state of peripheral vaso-dilation remains one of its most valid functions today.

Studies by Dr Mills of the Anchorage Medical Centre, Alaska, demon-strated the effectiveness of providing peripheral vasodilation 'on demand' as early as 1976 for frostbite victims. Once the patient is confident of his ability to produce the effect, the paraphernalia can be discarded. With very little experimentation, under the supervision of Dr Kappas who runs the bio-feedback clinic in Anchorage, I was able to record 4°-6°. I feel this contributed significantly to my ability to endure the extreme conditions we experienced, and I feel lucky not to have been amputated at the ankles and wrists. Mongol's naturally calm and placid temperament worked well in ensuring his survival.

The Indian Yogis took the root of certain species of the Rauwolfia plant for reasons other than warming themselves in the snow. They wanted to take advantage of the altered mood and feeling of relaxation to promote the meditative state that is associated with alpha-wave production in the brain. To a lesser extent, fresh ginger root and garlic cloves are thought to have a mild vasodilatory effect without carrying the problems of hyper-tension associated with the Rauwolfia root, or significant loss of core temperature. It can be a pleasant, harmless, and possibly useful addition to a climber's diet. Vasoconstricting effects of caffeine and smoking should be avoided, as well as the vasodilating effects of alcohol which can cause significant loss of core heat and induce or aggravate a state of hypothermia.

Why doesn't a wolf get frostbite? Look at it, standing in the snow, motionless, for long periods of time, stalking its prey in the middle of an arctic winter. To answer this question, physiologists discovered that the wolf has a highly developed facility for adaptating to cold. Most of the time the peripheral circulation is 'closed down' which helps maintain a high core body temperature designed to keep the vital organs — brain, heart lungs, liver, kidney and bowel — alive. At regular cyclic intervals, the peripheral blood vessels 'open up' and infuse the extremities with blood and oxygen, synonymous with warmth and life, without the wolf suffering significant loss of core temperature.

According to Dr Walkinshaw, assistant professor of plastic surgery, U.W. of Harbourview Medical Center, Seattle, it is thought that humans, when highly adapted to a cold environment, experience a similar phenom-enon called 'the Hunting response'. His theory is that the sudden and severe deep freezing episode I experienced with my hands may have caught me 'off cycle', i.e. when my peripheral circulation was closed down. At the same time I recognised the signs of cerebral oedema in Chris, giving me a sudden boost of adrenalin. This system works most of the time to a greater or lesser degree, but other associated phenomenon i.e. exhaustion, dehydration etc. may cause a breach in the mechanism which at other times would still be functional. Profound dehydration followed during the lengthy evacuation of four and a half days to Base Camp, half of which was spent without any fluid at all. When I did drink I vomited it back up, making the situation grim.

I was forced to remove my outer gloves and just wear glove liners to perform any kind of manipulation and give some degree of dexterity for tasks such as tying up crampon straps and boots after the fingers had frozen into rigid claws. This made it impossible to save my fingers, but then my instincts were driving me to save the body. The hands would be taken care of later.

One of the most frequent questions asked when people looked in horror at my mummified, charred, black fingers was, 'How cold was it?' In the absence of a thermometer all I could answer was 'pretty cold', or 'cold enough to break metal'. They would leave the room muttering something about 'wind chill factor' — a term used to describe the rate of heat loss by convection. In actual fact, at the time of the freezing episode, the weather was partly cloudy but little wind was present. According to the chart on page 10 of *Hypothermia, Death by Exposure* by Wm W. Forgey, if my fingers froze in less than 30 seconds (they froze solid in a matter of a few seconds) the temperatures must have been in the range of −60°F to −75°F. Many people think, incorrectly, that objects left outside will assume the temperature of the wind chill equivalent. For instance, if the ambient temperature is above freezing, it is impossible to get frostbite in spite of how hard the wind blows.

This discussion is not intended to be definitive, but merely to present observations and insights into some of the factors involved that can tip the delicate balance from safety to disaster.

Standard protocol for treatment by rapid thawing in warm water and avoidance of refreeze/dryheat, should be followed. *Hypothermia, Death by Exposure*, by Wm W. Forgey is highly recommended reading.

Mongol's frostbite injuries were less severe in that on both hands, thumbs and index fingers remained unaffected. Varying levels of amputation resulted on his fingers to the middle joint — his right hand more than his left. He kept his gloves and mitts on the entire time, to my knowledge. On his foot both big toes are amputated to the ball of the foot and varying amounts remain of the others toes. He also sustained frostbite of his left and right heels. The exact level of his disability will become more apparent as he tries to resume work. He was fortunate to be paid a small disability insurance and, with the combined financial aid of myself and some of his previous employers from other trips, he has managed to get by under difficult circumstances. Doug and Jan Scott generously arranged a trip to England, and he stayed with them for several months.

Given the language difficulties it is hard to discern how Mongol feels deep down about what happened, Doug sums it up thus: 'It was a bad thing that happened, but out of that some good has come. He got to take a trip to England, France and Ireland and meet a lot of his western friends from previous trips.'

APPENDIX B

I first knew and climbed with Chris when he was a medical student. It was at that time that I sensed an unusual combination of prodigious strength and joy coupled with a renegade but not foolish sense of adventure. Everyone around drew from his strength, and he always carried others with him to the summit. In 1976 he asked me to join him on the American Everest Expedition. Work would not allow me to go, but it was clear that Chris wanted help with the medical chores since his climbing ambitions were primary. His success on that expedition is history and is a tribute to the fact that he would not settle for second best. The 'ordinary' way was not for him.

It is, therefore, understandable that he and Cherie should attempt a bold climb in keeping with the advancing standards of today's Himalayan climbing. It is also clear that theirs was a relationship that drew on each other's strengths, and a conquest of Kanchenjunga would need that. Their 'near' success came from commitment to each other and to the task at hand. Having the privilege of getting to know Cherie after her return, I feel that they had this symbiotic relationship without which the undertaking of such a climb would not have got them above 5,400 m (18,000 ft). Some insight into their joy can be gained by passages in the last chapters during the most desperate of times: 'This was what we were meant to be doing...we were where we wanted to be.' These lines ring of Maurice Herzog's words from his classic book *Annapurna*, written when he and his team were testing the barriers of Himalayan climbing in 1950: 'We were on the mountain of our dreams.' One of my high altitude scientific colleagues, Sukhamay Lahiri, has said, 'Reality is according to dreams', and for Herzog, Cherie and Chris, reality, germinated in dreams, extracted a high price of life and limb. But we dare bravely because we must, for without the burden of dreams there is nothing for which to live.

I therefore feel it is out-of-place to comment on the 'advisability' of alpine Himalayan ascents. There is little to no margin of safety or recourse to help, but there are certain precautions which can allow us to approach our dreams without embracing total foolishness. Cherie's account demonstrates that both she and Chris possessed a sophisticated level of knowledge of the afflictions of high altitude illness and that they were careful to watch for the first signs of mountain sickness. Tragically, some of these signs are unpredictable and rapid in onset. In addition, keeping vigilance on the signs of deterioration of health at high altitude becomes difficult when the mental acuity to do so becomes obfuscated by the effects of hypoxia (low oxygen) on the brain. Regardless of this fact, Cherie's lucid account and Chris's clarity the day before his death would belie the suspicion that they were not watching for the signs of altitude illness. It seems to me that

Chris's high altitude pulmonary (HAPE) and cerebral oedema (HACE) were more like an avalanche than an insidious deterioration in the weather. Let us review the situation with respect to altitude illness to try and clarify what has heretofore been but speculation.

First, the best treatment of altitude illness, whether it be the mild, self-limited variety of headache and malaise or the potentially fatal variety of pulmonary and cerebral oedema, is prevention by slow acclimatisation during ascent. If one reviews the ascent profile of their climb it seems clear that more than adequate time was allocated for adaptation, if only by dictation of the weather. True acclimatisation probably cannot occur over 5,400 m (18,000 ft) but the 13 nights at Base Camp (5,000 m/16,800 ft) and 22 nights at Camp 2 (6,000 m/20,000 ft) certainly allowed for optimal adaptation, if not true acclimatisation. One could question whether slow deterioration at 6,000 m (20,000 ft) could have contributed to subsequent acute illness, but the ascent profile is not atypical of many which lead to success on 7,800 m (26,000 ft) peaks. The final push to the summit was necessary in the light of waning physical, mental, and logistical resources. Additionally, there is some evidence to suggest that certain adaptations of the red blood cells' capability to pick up oxygen at the lung and deliver it to the tissues may be optimised by a period of acclimatisation at modest altitude followed by a push to extreme altitude. Other factors, though, are important to consider.

Nutrition and hydration are crucial elements in success and survival on 7,800 m (26,000 ft) peaks. Being above 6,000 m (20,000 ft) results in a slow breakdown of muscle mass, and repeated forays to higher altitudes results in even further deterioration. Attempts to stay well nourished are usually thwarted by conditions and loss of appetite, so it seems clear that more than 40 days above 5,400 m (18,000 ft) resulted in loss of strength for Cherie and Chris — an inevitable consequence of Himalayan alpine climbing. Cherie writes about their continual attempts to melt snow to stay hydrated in order to optimise blood flow to vital organs and muscle mass, not to mention the brain. Extraordinary fluid losses occur because of the marked hyperventilation and dry air, such that remaining well hydrated is near impossible. It is generally accepted that compulsive drinking of liquids minimises predisposition to altitude illness. Cherie and Chris appeared to follow as best as possible these guidelines.

Were there any warning signs that Chris had impending cerebral and pulmonary oedema? What about the bloody sputum? Climbers with overt and severe HAPE may have bloody, frothy sputum which is a sign that the lungs are at least partially filled with bloody fluid which impairs the transfer of oxygen from the air to the blood and leads to worsening hypoxemia (low oxygen in the blood) and eventually death. Cherie's description of Chris's strong climbing and good spirits the day before he died makes the existence of HAPE or HACE on that day near impossible.

My experience with HAPE and HACE on Mount Everest and Mount McKinley is that climbers have trouble ambulating on the level, let alone on an incline. It is also extremely unlikely that the bloody sputum was a result of a blood clot in the lung — a condition that is well described in high altitude climbers. This clinical syndrome also results in marked respiratory distress which Cherie does not describe in Chris. The bloody cough was, therefore, probably just from dried and irritated mucous membranes in the upper airways.

What about Chris's cough and sputum? Chronic cough and sputum production secondary to the irritating effect of hyperventilation in cold, dry air is almost universal at high altitude. This condition can be incapacitating and is made worse by smoking, which Chris did, but here again it is unlikely that this condition was a major predisposing factor to his illness.

Blurred vision and confusion while climbing at extreme altitude is thought to be secondary to brain hypoxia. These symptoms can abate with rest, although if the hypoxemia is profound enough there can be sustained visual and cerebral dysfunction. Small haemorrhages in the back of the eye are quite common at altitudes above 5,100 m (17,000 ft) and may in and of themselves be sources of blind spots. More ominously, they may reflect what is going on in the brain. Cherie does not describe either of these problems until the morning of Chris's death by which time he was profoundly ill. So here again, there were no warnings.

Did the stove play a role in his illness? Burning stoves give off carbon monoxide which competes with oxygen in the red blood cell and thereby decreases oxygen delivery. But on the day of Chris's decline Cherie describes an extinguished stove probably giving off irritating propane fumes which may have resulted in wheezing and spasm of airways to make breathing more difficult.

The scenario that best fits the situation to me is that Chris was basically as healthy as one can be in this environment until the night before his death. HAPE and HACE struck suddenly, not atypically at night when breathing is lower, leading to lower oxygen levels in the blood. This suppressed breathing can be worsened by sedatives and sleeping pills, but we have no record that Chris was using these medications. Sleeping pills used to be quite popular at high altitude where sleep is difficult, but we have noted on Mount McKinley and elsewhere that there is an association between sedatives and the development of HAPE and HACE. They are, therefore, potentially very dangerous. Furthermore, Chris's strong climbing history throughout his life gives us no hint that he would be predisposed to becoming ill, but at these heights HAPE and HACE can strike even the most seasoned, previously healthy climbers. Hypoxemia worsens because of increasing fluid in the lungs, and brain function deteriorates because of profound lack of oxygen.

In spite of taking every reasonable precaution and making careful observations, Cherie and Chris were in an arena of very high risk with little or no recourse to help. Their commitment to each other and to the climb nearly brought them success. But fate would have it otherwise, and Cherie's and Mongol's valiant efforts to save Chris were futile. They were lucky themselves to survive the descent without loss of life but the struggle to survive triumphed, and Cherie returned to tell a tale of courage, love, joy and tragedy. May we all draw from their commitment to a goal where the stakes are so high.

Robert B. Schoene, MD
Associate Professor of Medicine
Division of Respiratory Diseases
University of Washington, USA

APPENDIX C

ITINERARY OF KANCHENJUNGA CLIMB

1984

25 November	Left Ghunsa after 3 days at 4,000 m (13,000 ft).
28 November	Arrive Pang Pema, spend 2 days acclimatising at Base camp, 5,000 m (16,800 ft).
1 December	Load carries to, 5,500 m (18,500 ft). Sleep at 5,000 m (16,800 ft).
2 December	Load carries to, 5,500 m (18,500 ft). Sleep at 5,000 m (16,800 ft).
3 December	Rest day at 5,000 m (16,800 ft).
4 December	Load carries to 5,500 m (18,500 ft). Sleep at 5,500 m (18,500 ft).
5-6 December	I stay at 5,500 m (18,500 ft), (rock falls on leg). Chris and Mongol route to 6,000 m (20,000 ft). Sleep at 5,500 m (18,500 ft).
7 December	Rest day for all at 5,500 m (18,500 ft).
8 December	3 loads to 6,000 m (20,000 ft).
9 December	Rest day 6,000 m (20,000 ft).
10 December	To base ice gully 6,150 m (20,500 ft). Return due to bad weather. Sleep at 6,000 m (20,000 ft).
11 December	Route through gully up to 6,300 m (21,000 ft) (cache). Return due to bad weather, sleep at 6,000 m (20,000 ft).
12-14 December	Rest days due to bad weather, 6,000 m (20,000 ft).
15 December	Return to Base Camp, rest.
16-18 December	Base Camp, rest.
19 December	3 loads to 6,000 m (20,000 ft) from 5,000 m (16,800 ft).
20 December	Rest day at 6,000 m (20,000 ft).
24-25 December	Rest days at 6,000 m (20,000 ft) due to bad weather (high winds).
26 December	3 carries to 6,800 m (22,800 ft), cache and return to 6,000 m (20,000 ft) due to bad weather (high winds).
27-30 December	Remain at 6,000 m (20,000 ft) waiting out bad weather.
31 December	Carry to 7,000 m (23,000 ft), retrieve caches, sleep in crevasse.

1985

1 January	Return to 6,000 m (20,000 ft), more bad weather.
1-5 January	Base Camp 5,000 m (16,800 ft), rest and wait out bad weather.
7-9 January	Return to 6,000 m (20,000 ft), more bad weather.
10 January	Arrive 7,000 m (23,000 ft), sleep in tent.
11 January	Stay at 7,000 m (23,000 ft) due to bad weather.

12 January	Bivvy middle rock band 7,100 m (23,700 ft).
13 January	Sleep in tent above rock band, 7,200 m (24,000 ft).
14 January	Highest point approx. 7,800 m (26,000 ft). Sleep in cave.
15 January	Descend am, Chris dies approx. 7 pm at 7,500 m (25,000 ft).
16 January	Descend to 7,200 m (24,000 ft).
17 January	Descend to 7,000 m (23,000 ft).
18 January	Descend to 6,300 m (21,000 ft).
19 January	Arrive at Base Camp, 10.30 pm.

TOTAL NUMBER OF NIGHTS SPENT AT EACH ELEVATION ON ASCENT OF KANCHENJUNGA

Approximate Height	Camp	No. of nights
5,000 m (16,800 ft)	Base Camp	13
5,500 m (18,500 ft)	Camp 1	6
6,000 m (20,000 ft)	Camp 2	22
6,800 m (22,800 ft)	Camp 3	3
7,100 m (23,700 ft)	Bivvy rock band	1
7,200 m (24,000 ft)	Camp 4	1
7,800 m (26,000 ft)	Bivvy Camp 5	1

APPENDIX D

I would like to credit Adams Carter for compiling the information (see Classification of Himalaya American Alpine Club Journal Vol. 27) and Dr Harka Gurung and Dr Ram Krishna Shrestha, two Nepalese scholars, who did an inventory of all the peaks above 6,000 m (20,000 ft) with the latest altitudes and corrected names. They used primarily the Survey of India topographic sheets at a scale of 1 inch to 1 mile (1.63, 630). They also used maps at 1:50,000 prepared for the Sino Nepalese Boundary Agreement 1979.

Kanchenjunga	8,586 m	(28,168 ft)
Yalung Kang	8,505 m	(27,903 ft)
Kangbachen	7,903 m	(25,927 ft)
Kumbhakana (Jannu)	7,710 m	(25,294 ft)
Kirat Chuli (Tent Peak)	7,365 m	(24,165 ft)
Gimmigela I (Twin I)	7,350 m	(24,144 ft)
Gimmigela II (Twin II)	7,005 m	(22,982 ft)
Pathibhara (Pyramid Peak)	7,123 m	(23,370 ft)
Ramthang Chang (Wedge Peak)	6,812 m	(22,350 ft)
Drohmo I (East)	6,886 m	(22,590 ft)
Drohmo II (West)	6,559 m	(21,520 ft)
Makalu	8,463 m	(27,766 ft)
Chamlang	7,319 m	(24,012 ft)
Baruntse	7,129 m	(23,390 ft)
Everest (Sagarmatha)	8,848 m	(29,028 ft)
Lhotse	8,516 m	(27,940 ft)
Lhotse Shar	8,400 m	(27,559 ft)
Ganchimpo (Gangchenpo) in Jugal Himal	6,387 m	(20,954 ft)

One of my difficulties when writing this book was in deciding how to spell Kanchenjunga. After considerable vacillation I opted for the spelling chosen on our 1981 Expedition and used on all stationery, T-shirts etc. This does contradict the most recent spelling, Kangchenjunga, recommended by HMG of Nepal. I apologise for adding possibly to further confusion.

APPENDIX E

SPONSORS AND EQUIPMENT SUPPLIERS

EQUIPMENT DONATIONS:
Recreational Equipment Inc.
Johnson Camping Co. Inc.
Skyr Underwear
Dolt of California
Innovative Sports
Koflach Footware
Kaufman Footware
Reichle USA
Mountain Travel USA

FOOD DONATIONS:
Galileo Capri Salami Inc.
Tang
Golden Grain Macaroni Co.
R.T. French Co.
Carnation Milk
MJB Quick Brown Rice
Cambridge Bars
Vella Cheese Co.
Star Kist Tuna
Sunshine Biscuits
Sunmaid Growers of California
Hershey Chocolate Co.

GLOSSARY

Anchor	The point to which a fixed line or belay line is attached to the mountain either by a piton, ice screw, ice axe or 'dead man', or a natural feature such as a rock spike.
Assender	See jumar.
Base Camp	Point at which organisation of equipment and supplies takes place.
Belay	Method of safeguarding one's rope partner from falling by tying oneself to an anchor point.
Bergschrund	The gap or crevasse occurring in a glacier when the slope changes angle to the mountain proper and rises steeply. The upper lip will often overhang the lower lip.
Bilge	Part of a boat which lies below the waterline.
Bilge hose	Hose through which water passes from bilge.
Bilge pump	Pump, either hand or electric, used to empty water from bilge.
Binnacle	Protective housing that mounts a compass.
Bivouac (bivvy)	Temporary sleeping place on a mountain without a tent.
Bowsprit	A large spar projecting forward from the stem of a vessel (see diagram, page 11).
Bulkhead	A wall dividing the boat into sections which also gives the hull and deck structural strength.
Cache	Supplies left temporarily on route before a camp is established.
Chock	Type of anchor that is lodged in a rock crack.
Choinard	Brand name of high quality climbing equipment.
Col	Lowest point on a ridge, usually between two higher points or peaks.
Couloir	An open gully.
Crampons	Steel spikes with frames that are fitted to a climbing boot. The sharp spikes provide a grip for ice and hard snow.
Crevasse	A fissure in the surface of a glacier that is formed when the glacier flows over an irregular surface bed causing tension and pressure differences. It can be very wide and deep and/or disguised by heavy snow cover.
Croissant	Name given to arc-shaped band of rock base or summit pyramid on Kanchenjunga.
Cwm	A rounded hollow surrounded by snow and ice, usually at the end of a glacier.

'Dead man'	A plate of alloy which is dug into the snow as an anchor. It digs in deeper the harder it is pulled.
Depth sounder	Instrument used to measure depth of water by sound waves.
Doghouse	A small cabin on deck which provides protection.
Down loft	Goose down, to date, is considered the lightest, warmest material for providing insulation against the cold. The thickness of the down (or loft) is a measure of how much warmth will be provided. Unfortunately it compacts quickly when wet or even damp.
Drogue	Ropes or chain trailed behind a vessel to slow her down and prevent surfing down large swells.
Eyebolt	Fixture, bolted in place, designed for tying line or shackles.
Fixed rope	Rope that is secured by anchors to the slope, after the person going first has run out the required length of rope. It is usually used over very steep terrain, and left in place for the duration of the climb. Subsequent climbers, by clipping into the rope with a jumar, can then move up and down the slope independently and be safeguarded from falling.
Fo'c'sle	The forward section below deck at the bow of a boat.
Foredeck	The forward section on the deck of a boat.
Gaff jaw	Fixtures designed to hold a spar snug to the mast of a gaff-rigged vessel (see diagram, page 11).
Gortex	Brand name of waterproof synthetic material that is said to 'breathe', eliminating the problem of condensation.
HACE	High altitude cerebral oedema.
HAPE	High altitude pulmonary oedema.
Headsail	A sail used ahead of the mainsail of a boat on a sloop or ketch-rigged vessel.
Hull	The main body of the boat.
Hypothermia	Generalised cooling of body temperature to below 35°C (95°F) — mild, 32°–28°C, (90°–83°F) — moderate, or below 28°C (83°F) — severe. Clinical signs and symptoms such as changes in personality, uncoordination, slurred speech, can occur with only a two to three degree drop in temperature.
Hypoxia	Lack of sufficient oxygen to the tissue.
Ice axe	Basic tool of the mountaineer. It provides balance on steep ground, purchase on hard snow and ice, it is used

	as a belay and to stop oneself when falling.
Jumar	A clamp that is attached to a rope and slides upwards. When weight is put on it, however, it remains fixed in place.
Karabiner	Oval metal snap links used for many purposes including tying the climber to an anchor.
La	Tibetan word for a pass.
Lee	Covered or sheltered side from wind and weather.
Liaison officer	An official, usually from the police force, appointed by the Government of Nepal to facilitate relations between expedition members, staff porters and local people. He also ensures that the rules of mountaineering, as set down by the Department of Tourism's Division of Mountaineering, are followed.
Loam	Soil consisting mainly of clay, silt and organic matter.
Mainsail	The sail that is situated in the centre of a ketch rig or sloop rig (see diagram, page 11).
Mizzenmast	Mast aft and lower (on a ketch rig) of sailing vessel (see diagram, page 11).
Moraine	Accumulation of rocks and boulders carried down by a glacier.
Pitch	A section — usually the length of one 100 m (328 ft) rope — between two belay points.
Piton	A metal peg that is used as an anchor by hammering into the crack of a rock.
Polybottle	Plastic bottle.
Poop deck	Raised aft section of a boat.
Porters	Local people hired to carry loads to Base Camp.
Protection	The number and soundness of running belays used to make a pitch safer to lead.
Rakshi	Distilled spirit usually made from rice.
Rappel	Method of quickly descending steep terrain by sliding down the rope.
Sardar	Head man.
Sherpa	An ethnic group of mountain people whose origins are said to be Tibetan. Over the past 35 years they have become legendary for their important role as load carriers in high altitude mountaineering.
Skiff	A small, flat-bottomed, open boat.
Slough	To cast off or shed (as the top surface of snow in an avalanche).

Snowfluke	See 'dead man'.
Spindrift	Loose powder snow carried by wind or avalanche.
Staysail	The sail in front of the mainsail and behind the headsail on a ketch rig (see diagram, page 11).
Taffrail	A rail that contains the poop deck.
Tang	Brand name for an instant orange drink mix.
Tiller	A lever used to turn a boat's rudder, giving steerage.
Turnbuckle	Used to tighten down the rigging that holds the masts of a boat erect.